THE ANATOMY OF THE CLITORIS

THE ANATOMY OF THE CLITORIS
Reflections on the Theory of Female Sexuality

Anne Zachary

Routledge
Taylor & Francis Group

LONDON AND NEW YORK

First published 2018
by Routledge
2 Park Square, Milton Park, Abingdon, Oxon OX14 4RN

and by Routledge
711 Third Avenue, New York, NY 10017

Routledge is an imprint of the Taylor & Francis Group, an informa business

Copyright © 2018 by Anne Zachary

British Library Cataloguing-in-Publication Data
A catalogue record for this book is available from the British Library

Library of Congress Cataloging-in-Publication Data
A catalog record has been requested for this book

ISBN: 978-1-78220-525-8 (pbk)

Typeset in Palatino LT Std
by Medlar Publishing Solutions Pvt Ltd, India
Printed and bound by CPI Group (UK) Ltd, Croydon, CR0 4YY

For
Jean Rosemary 1927–

History shows a full gallery of feminine prototypes, many
of whom embrace the phallic emblem, and thus arose the queen,
the goddess, the cruel woman, who are all far from Freud's
poor melancholic submissive one

—Alcira Mariam Alizade

Interminable virgin lands are waiting in silence for
someone who is daring enough to reveal them

—Alcira Mariam Alizade

CONTENTS

vii

Part II

Part III

LIST OF CHARTS AND ILLUSTRATIONS

ABOUT THE AUTHOR

Dr Anne Zachary is a fellow of the British Psychoanalytic Society and fellow of the Royal College of Psychiatrists. She has had a thriving psychoanalytic practice for nearly thirty years.

Her NHS training in psychotherapy was at the Cassel Hospital and afterwards she spent eighteen months in a locum consultant post at the Maudsley Hospital. From 1988 to 2010 she worked part-time as an NHS consultant at the Portman Clinic, Tavistock & Portman NHS Trust, specialising in sexual perversion, violence, and delinquency. During this time, she was also seconded at different times to various medium-secure settings and for five years (2003–2008) to the high-secure setting, Broadmoor Hospital.

The topics that have inspired her to write tend to be controversial or "on the edge", either in terms of their subject matter as described above and including homosexuality, or because they span the interdisciplinary boundary, for instance psychoanalysis and biology, or psychoanalysis and law.

Since her retirement from the NHS, she has expanded her psychoanalytic practice and has determined to write more.

FOREWORD

Anne Zachary's book is, as its title suggests, an anatomy lesson, but because she is a psychoanalyst, and although she does not exactly say so, a feminist, this is a lesson with much more than an anatomical purpose.

Her purpose is to contest and, if possible, put right a century or more of psychoanalytical misunderstanding of the female body and therefore also of the female psyche. Psychoanalytic writing since Freud has had a great deal to say about the penis. Castration anxiety (in males and females), penis envy (attributed to females), and the phallus in its various guises (both penis and yet more or less than this)—the arguments about its pre-eminence go on and on. But where, asks Zachary, is the clitoris in this literature, and in psychoanalytic discourse more generally? Much of the time, she says, it is absent, or is merely present in a vestigial form, like a common conception of the organ itself. She describes historical moments when biologists and psychoanalysts have tried seriously to think and write about this subject. But in her view, their efforts for the most part failed to hold the ground they had taken, and the topic has then been returned to its previous obscurity.

Anne Zachary is well qualified to have taken on the anatomical dimension of these issues, since she first trained as a medical doctor, before she became a psychiatrist and a psychoanalyst. She is not discomfited or embarrassed by anatomical issues. In fact, one of the fine qualities of this book lies in its author having found an entirely unembarrassed and clear-headed, yet warm and personal tone of voice in which to address her contentious and, for some, disturbing or salacious subject. Her central anatomical argument—if a Foreword is to say anything, it seems unavoidable to put in a few words on what this is—is that the biological structure and function of the male penis and female clitoris are in most significant respects the same. Their main differences of visibility and size arise from the necessity to arrange the female genitals to permit babies to be conceived and born. This does not affect the similarities of the vascular, neural, and muscular complexity and circuitry of these parallel organic systems. The difference between them is that for the clitoris connectedness is internal, and therefore invisible to sight. But with the male genitalia too, not all is on the surface, since the prostate is hidden. The psychological and wider socio-cultural significance of Zachary's anatomical argument is to establish the parity between the nature and functional importance of the male and female organs in which much of the experience of sexual desire and satisfaction is physically located.

The author describes a body of recent scientific work by biologists who have discovered these anatomical and physiological facts. Yet, as she points out, the situation is more complicated than the term "discovery" implies. It is not the case that new depths or specialised regions of scientific knowledge—for example, from neuroscience or genetics— had to be drawn upon to produce these advances in understanding. It seems rather that already-established anatomical knowledge, even from medieval times, and skills—for example of dissection—enhanced by modern scanning techniques, were all that were needed to reveal these findings again. It seems to have been mainly a matter of looking in the right place, and ceasing to avert the scientific gaze. The psychoanalytic ideas of disavowal, and the related sociological concept of denial—even the misperceptions that follow from ideologies—seem to be far more relevant to understanding this history of not-knowing, and of fitful recognition followed by renewed forgetfulness, than deficits in the resources of biological science.

This book provides a brief but valuable history of psychoanalytic contributions to the understanding of female sexuality. One significant aspect of this story concerns the nature of the riposte that Melanie Klein and her mainly female colleagues made to the patriarchal theories of Freud, which despite his enlightened understanding of bisexuality as a universal psychological propensity, still seemed to see females as traumatised by what they do not possess. The counter-emphasis in Kleinian thinking was on the female's capacities to bear and feed children, which were just as liable to be a source of envy and jealousy in males as the absence of a penis is for females. But this argument went only some of the way to resolving the problems left by Freud's phallic approach. It succeeded in establishing a sphere of female parity, and even in some eyes more than this—how does the potency of the idle drone compare with the capability of the queen bee?—but at a cost of complicity with a diversion of attention away from female sexual desire and its locations in the body.

Certain contemporary social and cultural changes seem to be linked to the renewed attention now being given to these issues by Anne Zachary and other writers cited by her. It seems likely that it is the cultural emergence of a feminism based on the material independence of many women, and more common choices by them to defer childbearing or deliberately avoid motherhood, which have led to this renewed focus on female sexual pleasure and desire. Current concerns about the prevalence of female genital mutilation (FGM)—clitoridectomy in surgical terms—also reflect this cultural change, in so far as it has now come to seem reasonable and necessary to include an undamaged potential for sexual pleasure within the sphere of universal human entitlements.

Zachary is a sensitive and experienced psychoanalyst and psychiatrist whose chosen specialism has been the treatment of perversions, violence, and delinquency. She is balanced and subtle in her discussion of the issues raised by her central thesis. She suggests, for example, that there is a homology between the anatomical differences of male and female sexual organs, and some corresponding psychological dispositions. A partly hidden and interior connectedness of the female anatomy is reflected in female understandings and representations of the world. Where males are linear, females are inclined to concentricity, cluster, and circularity, she suggests. This argument recalls Erik Erikson's description in *Childhood and Society* of differences in the way that little boys and girls characteristically play with bricks—he observed that boys build towers, and enjoy knocking them down; girls more often construct enclosures. Zachary asserts the value and importance of female, as well as male, aggression. Giving birth to a baby demands it, she writes, but she also notes that female aggression is liable to be hidden, and can be all the more destructive for taking that form. She has encountered a great deal of male abuse of women in her forensic psychiatric and psychoanalytical work, and does not minimise the damage it causes. But she also notes that the precipitating factor in many of the cases she has encountered was a decision by a woman to leave her male partner.

This is a very necessary, timely, and important book. It throws light on a topic that seems to have usually been treated with great circumspection, and, one might suggest, hidden anxiety. Anne Zachary reports that she has encountered encouragement, though laced with anxiety, and therefore rejection, in earlier efforts to publish on these questions. She also admits anxiety in the process of writing about them herself. Nevertheless, it may be realistic to suppose that attitudes to these questions are unlikely to be rapidly transformed, even by a book as calm, humanly interesting, and sympathetic in its approach as this one. Resistances as persistent as this to the recognition of reality are likely to have deep causes. While male domination and the subjugation of women and fear of their sexuality are certainly two of these, this may not be the whole story. Might it be that the different degrees of display and hiddenness of male and female sexuality, in both their anatomical and cultural forms, are also related to innate differences in the relative vulnerability of males and females to sexual enactments? While society and its moralists rightly insist that the responsibilities attendant upon the conception of babies are equal for the males and females involved, anatomy decrees that it is the females who bear nearly all of the risks.

Michael Rustin
Professor of Sociology at the University of East London;
Visiting Professor at the Tavistock and
Portman NHS Trust, and at the University of Essex;
Associate of the British Psychoanalytical Society; and a
Fellow of the Academy of Social Sciences

PREFACE

This book represents the culmination of a long journey that has taken place throughout my psychiatric and psychoanalytic career. Drawn to thinking about women, I struggled to publish, first a chapter revisiting the vulnerability of puerperal women[1] and particularly, a paper on the menopause[2] that took fifteen years to be accepted. At the time, the menopause was not talked about and had not really featured in the literature. At the millennium, during the enormous cultural changes that were going on, there was also paper on homosexuality.[3] I include it here because in this book I address how women are often listed together with, for instance, homosexuals or other disadvantaged or minority groups. At the time of the homosexuality paper, I had already embarked on my NHS speciality of perversion, violence, and delinquency, largely focused on men but including being witness to the pioneering work of Estela Welldon on female perversion. Meanwhile, in the 1990s, I was asked to provide a three-year cycle of lectures on female sexuality for the Institute of Psychoanalysis Introductory Lectures and Seminars. This set me reading extensively and when, also around the millennium, the revised anatomical interpretation of the clitoris with its surrounding structures as integral parts appeared in the general press, I wanted to put it together with my growing knowledge of the psychoanalytic literature on female sexuality. Thus, I thought I would try to integrate Freud's classical theory and all the subsequent challenges and attempts at new theory. After all, Gillespie had done a similar thing by publishing a paper in the *International Journal of Psycho-Analysis* on the physiological work of Masters and Johnson in the 1960s.[4]

But interdisciplinary work is particularly difficult, publishing rigours and restraints had increased, and controversy within the theory reigned. It was not yet time, as had been the case with my paper on the menopause. Also, it was difficult to find a sufficiently sharp focus for a journal paper. Hence I have written this book.

My journey has included a visit to Dr Helen O'Connell, a urologist in Melbourne, on my first visit to family in Australia in 2011. She is the main proponent of the recent understanding of the clitoris as a larger organ and was interested in my pursuit.[5] She regarded Freud as an opinionated man who did not understand women; both of these criticisms are probably true but in no way undermine his genius. He was still a man of his times.

This book provides neither answers nor a new, all-encompassing and definitive theory of female sexuality. But I would like the information and links put forward to be added to the 2003 commentary of Phyllis Tyson[6] where she reviews all the latest work thus far, commenting that Freud's "dark continent is no longer quite so dark. But a generally accepted, comprehensive and integrated approach to the theory of female development, psychology and sexuality has yet to emerge" (Tyson, 2003, p. 1119). She concludes that "In this time of building bridges to the other disciplines, we might do well to consider broadening and strengthening one *within* our own discipline—that is, between child and adult psychoanalysis" (Tyson, 2003, p. 1126). Whilst I agree with this wholeheartedly, my contribution to the bridge-building is more far-reaching and comes from the medical world of anatomy with an eye on history.

Moving to the specific topic of the book, here are some central quotations:

> The cleft vulvar anatomy is homologue[7] to its non-cleft male counterpart.
>
> (Van Turnhout, 1995, p. 767)[8]

> Modern anatomy textbooks have reduced descriptions of female
> perineal anatomy to a brief adjunct after a complete description of
> the male anatomy.
>
> (O'Connell, 1998, p. 1894)

I realise that what has caused much of the delay in completing this piece
of work is the potential pitfall for a psychoanalyst, albeit a psychoanalyst with a medical background, in taking as the starting point the
biological statements that have been made. A psychoanalytic response
might immediately be that this is a hysterical phenomenon, a chance to
say that male and female are the same, that the confusion about choice
is not an entity. Not only do I run the risk of declaring myself a hysteric
but, furthermore, it might be seen that I am adopting a phallic position
in order just to address these findings.

Kohon (1997) spells this out in his opening chapter on hysteria, at
first seeming to accentuate these risks and then to dispel them. What is
glimpsed are the lively workings of the oedipal complex and his chapter
is vital reading. Kohon also arrives at the conclusion I do, though from
a different angle, that Birksted-Breen's concept of "penis-as-link" (1996)
is too male in its name because, as he says, it is "connecting that which
is good to the male organ" (Kohon, 1997, p. 12). It seems necessary to
contribute from a biological point of view in terms of modern understanding to the concept of structuring, even though Birksted-Breen's
concept of "penis-as-link" is one of unconscious internal objects. The
unconscious is all-knowing, so it must "know" how the body is structured, more than we might be used to taking as a starting point.

The issue to be examined is that the clitoris is much larger than it is
commonly thought to be, with surrounding structures that encircle the
vagina to be included in its make-up. This is how it comes to resemble
the penis, though it has been evolutionarily adapted to accommodate
childbirth. The proposition of a transfer of erogenicity from the clitoris
to the vagina thus becomes less necessary. The conspiracy held throughout the centuries in order to control apparently infinite feminine desire
and capacity for pleasure that for many has led to loss of vaginal feeling
can be properly addressed.

In their own right, these biological findings have been made using
classical dissection skills, painstakingly recorded in anatomical drawings and backed up by modern scanning methods. Then they have been

peer-reviewed and published in journals within the field of urology. It is essential to find a forum in which to examine these findings without using our own theory to throw them out, or rather to avoid them, before there has even been a chance to think about it. This is what I hope to provide and then to show. It is a beginning.

The authors of the works describing the biological findings are women. (Two out of three, Helen, Amelia. I have not been able to find the first name of A. van Turnhout.) But I do not believe this to be a female hysterical conspiracy; they are only reporting what they find, in the interests of womankind, and noting that such interpretation as theirs has been put forward before at different times over the centuries and then *removed*. Women will be interested in exploring their own anatomy, will be motivated to help to correct the sociological inequalities and injustices that arise from misinterpretation throughout history, some of which continue into the present.

It is scientific discovery and education that have reduced the incidence of disorders such as hysterical conversion: the limb that no longer works after firing the shots in war, the woman who cannot walk as a solution to pressure to become a sexual being. Perhaps the interpretation of the female genitalia being passed on in this book could be useful in addressing the current epidemic in the field of transgender disorders where surgical reconstruction is still an option and increasingly offered. Rather than challenging sexual difference that of course is a reality, this book presents a balance between the sexes, a clearer backdrop for the activity of the male and the receptivity of the female, another way of thinking about the theory of "complementarity" that I explore in the book (in Chapters Three and Four). I will think of "homologue" as "balance" as my exploration unfolds. It is possible that a greater balance can free up the theory.

A book arises out of a conviction. It has to be like that to weather the process. Convictions can be the basis of madness, the madness of a psychoanalyst arguing for a place for biology. I have learned much from struggling with this dilemma and hope that useful theoretical constructions can come from having entered such a passionate debate. In Chapter Seven, "Femininity: the key to the box", I feel it is possible to imagine this happening.

During the recent process of writing, as things seemed to keep staying afloat, I noticed that my dreams were particularly positive. I took this as a good omen, in memory of Harold Stewart, my long-time supervisor. He believed in paying heed to one's own dreams.

> I dreamt: that my mother recovered her youth and beauty. When the carers arrived in the morning, I went to the door saying, "You will not believe what has happened ... !"

If only that were possible, but at a symbolic level it represents for me what I hope the contents of this book represent for all women, past, present, and future, in terms of a greater cultural freedom and equality.

INTRODUCTION

Around the millennium, there was a sudden rush of interest in sexuality and extraordinary, culture-changing things occurred. For a powerful example we only have to look at the world of homosexuality and how, emerging humanised from the AIDs epidemic, behaviour changed and society became more accepting (Parsons, 2000b), leading to changes in the law and now allowing same-sex marriage.

This book will focus on female sexuality, which is often listed, together with homosexuality and other "minority groups", as a "second sex" (de Beauvoir); as the "faulty sex" (Angier). The history of womankind is briefly reflected upon in Chapter One. Female sexuality also received a burst of insight at the millennium. A series of seemingly unrelated international scientific papers appeared in the biological academic press, opening up the anatomical interpretation of the female genitalia in a most creative direction. A Swedish paper in *Acta Obstetricia et Gynecologica Scandinavica* (Van Turnhout, 1995) and an Australian one in the *Journal of Urology* (O'Connell, 1998) described the clitoris as being comprised of the classical glans *and* the surrounding bulbs of the vestibule, making it more similar in construction to the penis, shifting the focus of difference to the fact that it is mostly internal. Also, that this larger clitoris surrounds the vagina, a third opening besides the urethra and the bowel, evolutionarily adapted to provide the passage for both conception and birth. The scientific language is very stark and makes it sound as though male and female are being equated: "The clitoris is the homologue of the penis." In a helpful way, which underlines that male and female are still *not* the same, an Italian paper (Toesca, 1996) explained the difference of the female from the male, in the anatomy of the bulbs themselves, in terms of the structure of the veins involved in tumescence (Chapter Two). Discovering this Italian reference more recently helped me to create more space for thinking about theory and also gave me the idea of expanding what had been intended to be a paper into this book. This ended an impasse I had fallen into about how to achieve my project.

We are indebted to scientific journalists for bringing the biological understanding to our attention and for trying to open up the position of women from a physical standpoint. In the UK David Aaronovitch sometimes reports on female issues. I am not sure now where I first saw a newspaper report about the scientific papers on the clitoris. But around the same time he wrote a piece, "Unwanted orgasms" (The Independent 23/12/97). It publicized a recent article in *The Lancet* about male orgasms being directed by the primitive hypothalamus (also present in fish brains) while female orgasms belong to the higher brain and might still be evolving. (See the "fish ancestress," Gillespie's term from 1975, Chapter Two p. 19). Natalie Angier's book in the USA *Woman* (1999), addresses the subordinate place of women generally throughout history. This book is filled with solid scientific information but to my mind is written in an overly brash style. Unfortunately, it seems to me that these new-found creative contributions to a difficult area were not taken seriously and therefore did not lead to the same ground-breaking changes for women as there were, for instance, in the world of homosexuality. There are reasons for this that can be understood by taking the whole history of womankind into account (Chapter One). For instance, there is the universal fear of and therefore control of female desire. There is also the defensive representation of what Perelberg (after Kristeva) calls "the Abject" (2015, p. 165) with its dirty, religious, and second-class connotations.

Instead, the news was received with slight embarrassment that the clitoris should be "so large" and quickly confined to the tabloid press and late-night, lighthearted television programmes. The scientific and significant cultural implications were lost. This book aims to complement the journalists' well-informed and important contributions, as well as of course the original scientific work, calling upon a psychoanalytic approach to bring things together. I hope it will offer a more reflective response and more depth to the study of being female.

Psychoanalysis itself has had a controversial history in terms of the theory of female sexuality. The anatomical difference between male and female is easily evidenced by the external genitalia of the male. The female genitalia are hidden from view, and classically the clitoris is thought of as small and "vestigial". Therein lies the superficial basis of sexual inequality and any attempt to address it is taken as rivalry or envy. This was the trap Freud himself fell into with his theories of female sexuality that focused on penis envy and castration anxiety. His later theory of the repudiation of femininity did nothing to foster equality and rights, not yet so relevant in his day. Perhaps, it has been suggested, that because of his analysis of his own daughter Anna, he could not go along with Abraham (1920) and accept that the little girl in early infancy has an initial vaginal awakening of the female libido that is destined for repression (Cournut-Janin, 2003). Freud referred to female sexuality as "the dark continent" (1926e) which illustrates my themes.

During the last century, the feminists tackled radically the problems of inequality leading to access to rights. They put forward a reciprocal approach, the biological capacity for pregnancy and motherhood, evening things out sufficiently for a more creative appraisal of the *status quo*. In psychoanalysis, this was put forward by a number of female analysts (Horney, Deutsch, Benedek) and very much supported by Ernest Jones. Juliet Mitchell and Jacqueline Rose continued this discourse later. The debate was always stormy and passionate.

After the Freud–Jones debate of the first half of the twentieth century, a considerable body of literature built up, largely from the USA. But to my mind, there is a particular quality to the American literature that, if it does not begin to sound like the rather salacious, journalistic work, it becomes too "mumsy" (Balsam). She puts forward the idea of the patient's positive identification with the analyst's substantial bottom! In fact, it is searching for a definitive theory having adopted the idea of the identification with the mother originated by Jones et al.

In Chapter Three, I have compiled a grid in an attempt to capture a clear overview of the vast body of data. Most of the information is taken from Schuker and Levinson, *Female Psychology: An Annotated Bibliography* (1991, especially Chapter 18 on "Sexuality"). It is fascinating to see how throughout the century the discourse over the years takes on a quality that mirrors the subject matter itself. Ideas are presented, objected to, and then forgotten, only to re-emerge at a later date in a constantly circular pattern. Somehow this illustrates the nature of the female form itself: its concentricity; the hidden and secret female genitalia; the passion of the potentially insatiable desire that is so frightening; anxiety about the enormous capacity of the vagina to expand, even to the size of a baby during childbirth.

I am reminded of how in a similarly dynamic way institutions take on the characteristics of the pathologies contained within them. There is the sado-masochism of the institutional dynamics where the specialist interests are perversion, violence, and delinquency. (The Portman Clinic was famously renamed "the slaveship" by Harry Karnac when he was involved in the research there after his retirement from Karnac Books. It captured brilliantly not only the sado-masochism of the pathology it was treating but also how hard everyone worked.) Then there is the madness reflected in the containment of psychosis, or the sea of chocolate and flowers and celebration punctuated by moments of extreme grief in the maternity unit. Going back to the literature, of course the genius of Freud is that he illustrates the complexity of human nature without knowing all the answers, though sometimes predicting them, for example in his description of hormones before they were discovered in the 1920s (Freud, 1905d, p. 215). His careful documentation and the intensity of his complete works exemplify this throughout.

The new biological work on the clitoris at the millennium did not make it into the psychoanalytic literature. Using William Gillespie's model in his 1969 paper in the *International Journal of Psycho-Analysis* about the physiological work of Masters and Johnson on human sexual function, at the time I tried quite hard to introduce this information to the psychoanalytic world. The response to my communication was one of interest but further than that, to question its relevance, particularly to psychoanalytic theory and to find my attempts to convey it in a single paper too far-reaching. This is not surprising when, as one of my patients commented recently, having read Thomas Maier's book *The Masters of Sex* (2009), that the work of Masters and Johnson is still ground-breaking work today. Gillespie's model did not include clinical material. In a book, there is room for this, and I have provided some examples.

In Chapter Four, I have attempted to link the physical issues with how these can be represented psychically. As always, this is best done using clinical material, and it is rewarding to be able to find a place for my five-times-a-week research case from the Anna Freud Centre young adults' project. Miss K illustrates common difficulties experienced by young women as they approach adulthood and are confronted by their sexuality. So many do not fully realise their potential in this area. Miss K's analysis helped her to separate emotionally from her mother and to form a meaningful heterosexual relationship. This was against all odds, rigidly laid out by her at the beginning of the treatment.

What are the clinical implications of the re-interpretation of the structure of the clitoris? Chapters Five to Eight are a series of essays on topics relevant to womanhood: bisexuality, motherhood, femininity, and aggression. The anatomy of the clitoris is not the focus in these chapters but just something to be held in mind when thinking about the different aspects of womanhood. They are self-explanatory, but in writing them I began to find my way to what I really wanted to say and it is anchored in the essay on femininity.

Most people are physically explicit as either male or female. Bisexuality (Chapter Five), thought of by Freud as a universal phenomenon, refers then to the subjective experience of each individual as to exactly how male and how female they feel themselves to be. Theoretically, it is a psychical phenomenon rooted in the unconscious. My chapter offers clinical examples from two extremes, one biological and one psychological: those born as intersex (with androgen insufficiency syndrome, AIS) and mistakenly thought at birth to be female; and homosexual men with exaggerated female identification. These very vivid examples importantly serve to highlight issues relevant to us all to a lesser degree.

In Chapter Six on motherhood, I have concentrated on procreation as the biological aspect of motherhood as well as the transmission of love in a personal dedication to my own mother. My focus is on the concentricity of the intergenerational communication, structured in the unconscious by the evolution of the female sexual body to be formed in circles around a space for a baby to be conceived, nurtured, and born.

In theoretical terms, it is my belief that the book turns on the chapter on femininity, Chapter Seven, offering reasons why it has taken so long for the biology to be openly addressed by psychoanalytic theory.

Finally, aggression in women, the subject of Chapter Eight, can take on a characteristic quality very different from male aggression in the way that it is expressed. Reflecting the internal anatomy, it can be hidden, secretive, and as a result cruel. Of great importance, though, is also a positive aggression, for instance as required for childbirth and often repressed as not fitting into traditional terms of femininity.

The recent biological work examined cadavers that were new and unpreserved for greater accuracy. When I included this particular piece of factual information in my original accounts of the work, it provoked a strong reaction in one female reviewer. It was received as an unnecessary and aggressive affront to her sensibilities! "Did we have to have included …?" In retrospect, this kind of reaction probably set up an unconscious response in me which I think later led to my putting together the two halves of my title "Aggression and the female form" (Chapter Eight); I saw the response as a projection of the particular quality of female aggression that reflects the hiddenness of the female form or genitalia when I was only reporting scientific fact. Siobhan O'Connor described the same abhorrence of the detail in the preliminary responses to her "magnum opus" on female violence (2014) that appeared in *Psychoanalytic Psychotherapy* shortly before her death.

After the sudden flourish at the millennium, all seemed to go quiet again as if female sexuality went out of fashion in the literature. Chapter Nine looks at the latest literature. In a spot search, I found only one hundred and seventy-eight articles on women and female sexuality, nineteen of which I picked out as relevant here. Of these, six are reviews of Rosemary Balsam's book *Women's Bodies in Psychoanalysis* (2015). The other notable contribution is the dedication of much of an edition of the *Journal of the American Psychoanalytic Association* to women (2003), where many contemporary names in the American field—Tyson, Kulish, Balsam, Chodorow, and Kramer Richards—feature. Tyson begins with a commentary. She says:

> The mapping of this "dark continent" has preoccupied and perplexed psychoanalysis for more than three-quarters of a century, with the result that the continent is no longer quite so dark. But a generally accepted comprehensive and integrated theory of female development, psychology and sexuality has yet to emerge. Important controversies remain unresolved, poorly understood and some areas are still incompletely explored, poorly understood or in need of a fresh look.
>
> (Tyson, 2003, p. 1119)

Her colleagues I have listed above then take this fresh look, making an "important contribution toward the continually evolving and changing theory of the psychology of the female" (p. 1119).

At the same time, female psychoanalysts have been meeting together on a regular basis internationally. Examples of these are a British–French group and the Committee on Women and Psychoanalysis (COWAP) of the International Psychoanalytic Association. Interesting collections of work have been published as a result of COWAP, for instance *Notes on Femininity* (2003) and *Motherhood in the Twenty-First Century* (2006) edited by Alizade. Also, Raphael-Leff has edited *Female Experience* (1999) with Perelberg, and *The Female Body* (2013) was edited by Moislein Teising and Thomson-Salo. Each has written her own publications in the field.

Psychoanalysis is about the unconscious and its influence on behaviour. Its proponents strive with passion to protect the parameters concerning the mind and often actively reject any focus on the real body. This isn't always the case, and in the UK, Birksted-Breen represents those who take it into account. In the USA, Greenacre, so interested in bodily rhythms, says "thought is never really disembodied. One way or another thought bears the imprint of the accompanying body" (1964, p. 30). But I know a psychoanalyst who purports not to have a body! The renunciation is justified by saying that the body is studied in other appropriate disciplines and psychoanalysis has to protect itself. Whilst this is a valid point in some ways, it does not embrace the important opportunity to struggle at the boundary of body and mind because of course each influences the other, often unconsciously. Surely the way the body is understood in the modern world should influence how the mind is felt to relate to it. As always, to go back to Freud, he described the ego as a "bodily ego" (1923b, p. 26). I would advocate that psychoanalysis can gain from a discourse with other disciplines— "interdisciplinarity"—even though the language difference can be so difficult. It is important to struggle at the boundary. Wilson (1998) created a concept, "concilience", an effort to aid developments. This is beyond the scope of the aims of this book but serves here as a structure of support for further thinking.

The hypothesis that runs through my book is a simple one. How psychoanalysis has had evidence prior to the scientific re-discoveries of a different interpretation about the female body if it had only known it. Though Freud's own original theory of female sexuality is then left behind as old-fashioned, the pre-emptive unconscious knowledge that psychoanalysis can tap before science discovers it is yet another example, as happened with the discovery of hormones, that is so illustrative of Freud's genius. In the same way, Jones and his female colleagues, who would have needed him at the time to be heard at all, were in tune with the evolutionary development of an adaptive space for a baby, in their challenge to Freud.

At times throughout this book, partly because of my own professional background, my experience at the Portman Clinic with male and female patients, the theory of perversion comes to the fore. That women are often classed together with minority groups is a well- known phenomenon, and why that should be has many and complex historical, political, and cultural reasons, some of which I have addressed. Misunderstandings can occur, and perhaps it is wise to state that, for example, the hiddenness of the roots of perversion in the refraction through the Oedipus complex and loss of the meaning of the detail at puberty (Sachs, 1923), is not the same as the hiddenness of the female genitals, but might result from it. As an example, there is the theory of fetishism that also has its own substantial literature.

There is not space to acknowledge individually all the many patients, colleagues, and friends who have helped me to arrive at this debut of a book. I offer my warm thanks and gratitude to all. But I would like to mention especially Don Campbell for his encouragement early on; Anne-Marie Sandler and Gregorio Kohon for their interim support; Sheilagh Davies for her help with some crucial final adjustments; Saven Morris, librarian at the Institute of Psychoanalysis, for help with the referencing; Michael Rustin for help with my writing and for his valuable Foreword; Jane Milton, joint editor of *A New Dictionary of Kleinian Thought* and the Melanie Klein Archivist, for her special knowledge of Klein; Jeanie Carmichael and Katie Whyte for their helpful associations. I have chosen to dedicate the book to my mother Jean for reasons apparent in the chapter on motherhood and in my Afterthoughts. There is a second dedication to Alcira Mariam Alizade, whom I never met but whose writing really struck a chord and helped me to pull my own thoughts together in the chapter on femininity. Finally, I must acknowledge the superb behind the scenes support and encouragement from Karnac, particularly from Rod Tweedy throughout 2016 and more recently from Alyson Silverwood whose diligent and sensitive editing pushed me just that bit further.

I present this book in the interests of the theory of female sexuality moving forward in a constructive and useful way. Science informs where psychoanalysis was there already via the unconscious. We should feel proud of that and not feel that we have to defend ourselves against scientific creative achievements. I make a plea for psychoanalysis to take an interest in and not to reject new biological evidence. This is particularly relevant in neuroscience, but also especially in the field of female sexuality, since this evidence is all but pre-empted by various already-established psychoanalytic theories such as complementarity and concentricity. (Chapter Four) I hope to show how these theories reached out to understand how things might be different from how they appear, given the hidden and therefore naturally more secretive quality of female sexuality. This pre-emption is a feature that can only strengthen the position of psychoanalysis in the wider world.

I would like to say a word here about the book cover. I planned to use a flower painting of Georgia O'Keeffe, widely held to resemble the female genitalia and exhibited at the Tate Modern this year to mark the hundredth anniversary of her first exhibition. But apparently, she always lamented the fact that everyone viewed her flowers like this, and she tried to make them more and more accurate to show them as no-one else could see them. Instead, out of respect, I chose an abstract, *Green and Blue Music*. This illustrates the theory of synaesthesia, the stimulating influence of one sense upon another. To me, it serves to illustrate Toesca's anatomical work, the view that ended my impasse and freed up my thinking to go further with my own ideas.

Part I

CHAPTER ONE

Womankind through history

How to begin this book? I simply want to lay out the position women have found themselves in down the centuries and to create a template on which to explore the new attempt by anatomists, *fin de siècle*, to reconsider the biological interpretation of our make-up. Of course, here this concerns only the anatomy of the clitoris and a woman is made up of much more than this. But this aspect of woman may be extremely relevant not only socially but specifically in drawing together and developing psychoanalytic theory, my main aim of the book. What has happened is that the history of the development of knowledge of the female in other disciplines over history, and including psychoanalysis, has been governed by social and cultural mores and then suppressed.

The classical view of the history of the psychoanalytic theory of female sexuality is that it developed in the hands of one man, Sigmund Freud, and then passed into the hands of another man, Ernest Jones. Of course, it is more than implicit that Jones was the spokesman for a group of women, Horney, Deutsch, Benedek ... but even so, the Freud–Jones debate was a sign of those patriarchal times.

What is also important to recognise is that the development of the theory of psychoanalysis as a whole passed from Freud to two women,

Melanie Klein and Anna Freud. This important history is acknowl-
edged and described in terms very relevant to my approach now by
Margot Waddell. She chooses to focus on Klein. Having stated that
Freud concentrated on reconstructing the detail of past trauma and its
effect on present difficulties, she highlights Klein's work with children
and their interest "about inside matters—about what is going on inside
their own bodies and in those of their mothers" (Waddell, 1998, p. 2).
Taken up by Donald Winnicott also, the emphasis in theory had shifted
from biological drives to relationships. Later in this book, I will show
how that interest in the inside, the internal life of a person, in relationships, comes naturally to women when much of their sexual biology is,
in effect, inside.

There have always been powerful women who are remembered
down the ages: the Virgin Mary, Hildegard of Bingen, Joan of Arc,
according to Angier, thought to have possibly had androgen insufficiency syndrome (AIS) (see Chapter Five), Queen Elizabeth I ... But
none of these are remembered for their sexual pursuits. Queen Victoria
was a little different, her nine children with the love of her life Albert,
and then later her apparently very close friendships with one or two of
her male servants, her own private life to remain private. But ironically,
she was of an age when repression of sexuality for all was at a height,
and her name has since been given to mean just that, "the Victorian
era". None of these figureheads was representative, in the wider sense,
of all women by any means. Repression together with lack of education led to hysteria, psychosomatic complaints, pregnancies that were
dissociated from and denied. As far as the masses were concerned, the
women were the property of the men, they belonged to their fathers
and then to their husbands. In some cultures, there are still references to
the business side of marriage in the ritual of the ceremony. The dowry,
arranged between future husband and the bride's father, is a thing of
the not so distant past in Western culture.

Women were under the control of men throughout history—their
desire, their passion—their capacity for a limitless amount of these
inducing fear and restriction. There tended to be few pictures of their
beauty; they covered themselves to indicate modesty but also to minimise temptation. In some cultures, this still happens. Women were
second class, uneducated, seen as dirty, hidden in the home.

But there were renaissances. In medieval times, anatomical drawings existed and the larger, more natural dimensions of the clitoris as

an organ involving more of its surrounding structures were recognized. The drawings were banned. At the beginning of the twentieth century, according to Helen O'Connell, another series of diagrams of the female genitalia showing the clitoris was deleted from *Gray's Anatomy*, seen as unnecessary, unsuitable, or both. O'Connell tries at the end of the century to re-instate them. I will show, as the book goes on, how this same pattern of insightful ideas followed by their disappearance is repeated throughout the theory of psychoanalysis on female sexuality, coursing through the whole twentieth century.

In her first paper on the subject, O'Connell states that, "Since the studies of Masters and Johnson (1966) there has been surprisingly little investigation of basic female anatomy or physiology" (O'Connell, 1998, p. 1894). Her paper attempts to change the view that the clitoris is a "small knob" and to open up its larger three-dimensional structure incorporating the bulbs of the clitoris previously named the bulbs of the vestibule. She gives a detailed, anatomically accurate account of why this should be so (see Chapter Two).

There are many ways in which to indicate how the portrayal of women in different ages has fluctuated according to the culture of the times. Novels tend to be well researched and therefore informative. A novel set in Italy, *The Anatomist* (1998), by the Argentinian writer Federico Andahazi, recounts the true story of Mateo Renaldo Columbo's discovery of the clitoris, which he calls the "Amor Veneris" and which he had written up in *De re anatomica* (1559). (Andahazi draws an extravagant yet understandable parallel with Christopher Columbus' discovery of America. He is comparing the navigational anatomy maps for surgery with the navigational maps of the oceans.) Columbo, a renowned anatomist and doctor in Renaissance Italy, was put on trial by the Inquisition for the inclusion of this discovery in his book. For a flavour of the times—and every psychoanalyst will think of the superego—here is a quote from the novel, spoken by the Dean of the University:

> Are we to wait idly for these new painters, sculptors and anatomists to replace Our Lord Jesus Christ with marble statues of Lucifer above the pulpits?
>
> (Andahazi, 1998, p. 166)

Columbo is treating a wealthy and beautiful widow, Ines de Torremolinos, who was living in "Franciscan austerity" in Florence and who seemed to be dying of depression and lassitude. She is revived by his manual manipulation of her engorged clitoris. He gains a reprieve in court because, incidentally, he is meanwhile asked to cure the Pope of an illness and is successful. He wants to take his newfound knowledge back to his own love, a beautiful prostitute, Mona Sofia in Venice, but on finding her again she is already ravaged by advanced syphilis and she dies.

When Andahazi's novel was put up for the Forbat prize for literature, ironically it was denounced, setting up a scandal and charges of modern-day censorship. Irony indeed, here is another round of prohibition in another time, in tune with the theme of my book.

The novel begins as my book does, with the history. He recounts how before the sixteenth century not only were women's genitals hidden but women themselves were hidden. He begins: "The sixteenth century was the century of women …. Until (then) history had been recounted in a deep masculine voice." He quotes Natalie Zemon and Arlette Farge in their *History of Women*:

> Wherever one looks there she is, always present: from the sixteenth to the eighteenth century, always on the domestic, economic, intellectual and public stage, on the battlefront and in moments of private leisure, we find the Woman. Usually, she is busy at her daily tasks. But she is also present in the vents that build and tear apart society. From one end to the other of the social spectrum she occupies all places and those who watch her constantly speak of her presence, often with fear.
>
> (in Andahazi, 1998, p. 12)

Andahazi then explains how Mateo Columbo's discovery happened precisely at the moment when women who had always been indoors began to appear outside, "gradually and subtly … emerging from behind the walls of convents and retreats, from whorehouses or from the warm but no less monastic sweetness of home" (Andahazi, 1998, p. 13).

But the spiral continues. This was Renaissance Europe. I will digress here, and fast forward to the twenty-first century. Dubai is a very modern and rapidly expanded place that has little recorded history, since there was "nothing there" (some Bedouins and a few pearl fishers) until the discovery of oil in the middle of the twentieth century. In Dubai, there is a museum on the waterfront, a merchant's house. It is filled with beautiful black-and-white photographs of the original ruling family and other Bedouins, at home, out sailing and fishing, hunting with hawks in the desert. When I first saw these pictures, I was struck that they were all of men and boys. Where were the women? Of course, they were hidden, as they are still in public, behind their unkind black robes (unkind in the heat when the men wear white), but also hidden from the camera entirely, presumably at home. A few years later, I took my sister to Dubai and went back to the merchant's house, on the new visitors' list of places to see. I told her not to expect any pictures of women. We wandered through the rooms and right at the end, there were pictures of women. I don't think they were old, in fact many were in colour. Had I missed them before? If so, they were on the inside, at the end, relatively hidden, and I had missed those rooms. I hadn't really expected pictures of women if I thought about it, one always sees only what one sees and not necessarily what is there ... Or had they been added to bring the place into the present? Dubai is trying to be a very up-to-date place, and employs the world's best experts in everything. It is heartening to think that history can at least be added later!

To go back to Mateo Columbo. The scene is set with Mona Sofia at work in the bordello in Venice; Ines de Torremolinos, ill in Florence; and a black crow that Columbo has named Leonardino, which he allows to feed daily on the waste from his anatomy work in Padua. These three are called the "Trinity", while Columbo is the "Apex". At the end, the crow has become the Apex and the three humans are the Trinity. It is a rather enigmatic beginning and conclusion, difficult to know what Andahazi is meaning to convey. He is an psychotherapist. I think he means Ines to be the ego, Mona Sofia to be the id, and Leonardino the crow to be the superego. The crow certainly conveys foreboding in his blackness. But Ines has superegoish tones that are then overcome by the discovery of female pleasure and she becomes the id. Later (in 1599), she is burned at the stake. Mona Sofia, starting out as id, discovers only the risks of her profession, a real depressive position, but she has become the ego, then she dies of syphilis. The crow with his "voracious" appetite is yet patient and wise, despite being the primitive creature. He too suffers disappointment when the food supply comes to an end because Columbo is imprisoned, and he flies off to Venice, where Columbo will later find his own disappointment.

Andahazi presents his novel as "the story of a discovery" and "the chronicle of a tragedy". Columbo never saw his book in print. It appeared in 1599, the year of his own death.

How does this story help with developing my book? Literature can indeed be very helpful in transcending controversy and scandal arising in real life. There is a lot more to be gained from this novel (and its historical research) of relevance to my current task. An internet review suggests that "the depositions presented during the trial to show the evil and demonic nature of the good doctor are interesting for their links to the Salem witch hunt trials and to the Monica Lewinsky/ Clinton affair". It states that John Updike has observed that in all three situations the descriptions of what had gone on were far more explicit than would usually have been acceptable in each age. He called it "a sanctioned voyeurism". The complex theories of the creative process of perversion come into view, whether as the sexualisation of aggression, or the avoidance of psychosis, the disavowal of the woman not having a penis, the blurring of the boundaries of sexual difference and generational difference ....

Womankind; the kind of woman; the kind woman; all these terms indicate different aspects of the female persona. The kind woman mothers her children lovingly, supports her husband. But there is another kind of woman, described so importantly by Estela Welldon (1988), the mother who, should she be violent and/or vulnerable enough to act out her own negative feelings of envy, hate, neglect, that child will suffer because a mother is so dangerously close to her child. This particular quality of what Welldon termed "female perversion" is unbearable for society to contemplate.

But there is another kind of woman. If she can accept her own make-up, all its polarities of feelings good and bad, *integrate* them (according to those female analysts Payne, Brierley, Arden) and everything else that has to be negotiated in life, then there is the possibility of containment for the child. They see this as linked to her unconscious knowledge of her internal structures. To understand this as the evolutionary miracle that it is, rather than the poor second in size to the primary male, can only help. There is a parallel here with the Kleinian view of the resolution of the oedipal complex, but I am highlighting the Independent theory because it specifically speaks of women and their children.

A new book called *The Anatomical Venus*, text by Joanna Ebenstein (2016), highlights the change in interest, focus, challenges that goes on down the ages. It is an historical book documenting the preoccupations during the Age of Enlightenment in the eighteenth century: Europe ravaged by syphilis, women dying of consumption, the Catholic religion still reigning. It was heralded as a book about women, anatomy, full of photographs of the beautiful, and lifelike, wax models of women that were made during that era in an attempt to stop using cadavers to train doctors. (In the 1970s, we still used cadavers in London, in what was named the "Long Room", ten or fifteen bodies in rows as if in a morgue, eight medical students to a body, dissecting it for a whole year. The smell, the banter, the ethical issues … nowadays, I think there are more temporary preparations of parts of the body to dissect and video links to central laboratories.)

Thinking that *The Anatomical Venus* would enhance the background material for my book, I obtained it, and found it most informative and in some ways related—but to stick to my main focus, I was fascinated by what it left out. It is really a book combining art and history. The photographs are visually explicit, but in the whole of the text I could find only one reference to the actual anatomical detail, a description of a photograph showing a woman who had a congenital defect of her heart and this showed in the difference in the thickness of the walls of the ventricles (p. 115). Otherwise it was left to the eye and the main focus about women was that each wax effigy had a pregnant womb, usually a full-term foetus. Otherwise the actual genitals are not commented upon, and this will become very relevant in Chapter Seven of my book, "Femininity: the key to the box".

For now, a little more about *The Anatomical Venus*. According to Ebenstein, towards the end of the 1700s Clemente Susini created the "Medici Venus" in a wax workshop in Florence, a life-sized, anatomically correct, dissectible goddess of coloured wax which so resembles skin. She was beautiful because Susini took the idealised feminine beauty for which Italian artists had long been renowned.

> a perfect embodiment of the Enlightenment values of her time in which human anatomy was understood as a reflection of the world … to know the human body was to know the mind of God.
>
> (Ebenstein, 2016, p. 24)

But then, "her classically beautiful exterior and abject innards" (p. 131). Inside, the contents of her body were displayed in all their abjectness (compare Kristeva and Perelberg's word, the "Abject", when developing the psychoanalytic theory of female sexuality, see Chapter Four).

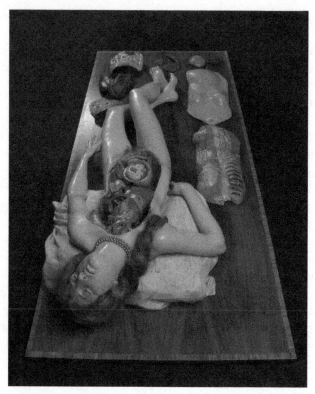

Figure 1. The *Venerina* (Little Venus), a dissectible, anatomical wax model made by Clemente Susini for the museum of Palazzo Poggi, Bologna, Italy (1792). Courtesy of Alma Mater Studiorum, Università di Bologna, Sistema Museale di Ateneo—Museo di Palazzo Poggi.

There were many of these wax anatomical Venuses. When introducing *The Anatomical Venus*, Ebenstein remarks that "the Anatomical Venus has come to seem so strange to modern sensibilities, a classic example of the uncanny" (p. 19). Later, she explores this, quoting Schelling, as Freud did for his essay on "The Uncanny" (1919), as Kohon did in his book on aesthetics (2016). "Uncanny" is what one calls something "that ought to have remained secret and hidden but has come to light" (Kohon, 2016, p. 11). This applies to the insides of a woman's body in the eighteenth century. This applies to the re-interpretation of the anatomy of the clitoris here (see particularly Chapter Seven). Kohon remembers that Freud: "maintained that the uncanny reveals the repression of a fear or trauma that had once taken place—more precisely, it would uncover the return

WOMANKIND THROUGH HISTORY   11

of the repressed threat of castration". But Kohon believes that this "does not exhaust the concept of the uncanny" (Kohon, 2016, p. 11), and he goes on to develop his theory of aesthetics and how psychoanalysis, art, and literature are not isolated: "Although they reveal different ways of feeling, modes of perception and styles of thinking, they are related in particular through the phenomenon of the uncanny" (Kohon, 2016, p. 21).

Documenting things from a scientific aspect, Angier is a fount of knowledge about all aspects of what she calls WOMAN (1999). As well as the anatomical discoveries I am highlighting, there is the situation at the cellular and the hormonal levels. She gives a very clear account of how the sex chromosomes, present in every cell of the body, determine (unless anything goes wrong) the sex of the individual. In every girl, there are two X chromosomes, one from each parent, each large and with large potential gene pools (most genes are switched off). In every boy, there is one X chromosome, always from the mother. How alike the boy will be to his mother! Is this another biological basis to the feminisation of the homosexual? Then the boy has a Y chromosome, denoting maleness, from the father. The Y chromosome is small with room for only thirty genes. It is high time that the smallness of the clitoris was confined to history, not only because it is inaccurate or shortsighted information, but because the size argument augurs badly, especially at the chromosomal level.

Topical at present is the issue of female genital mutilation (FGM). This is still carried out in some cultures and is beginning to be clamped down upon in civilised society. Schools are alerted to the situation of latency-aged girls receiving lavish presents before returning to their countries of origin for the long holidays. Practitioners of FGM in the UK are now liable for prosecution. It is a technique designed to control the girl's pleasure, in line with the social and cultural mores of the past; it is against human rights in the present day. Apparently, it is the women who arrange and even perform the ritual. I can only speculate that this is because they have been through the same and can only repeat the trauma; it must be based on an offering to cleanliness, ironically cancelled out if infection ensues; envy of a more liberated future; ignorance.

In the past, women have heaped pain and suffering on their daughters. In China, this was by binding their feet so that they stayed dainty and could not grow. This was a friend's association to reading this chapter, a lay insight into the theories of negation, the death instinct … She said,

"If the mothers did not pass on this suffering, it made their own misery pointless". There is a case history later in this book (in Chapter Four) of Miss K, who illustrates an unconscious link between the genitals and the feet, something repressed and restricted, displaced outwards and away down to the feet. Was this practice of foot-binding just another, more distant expression of the imprisonment of women by men, carried out by women, to impose sexual control? Having renounced her sexuality, my understanding of Miss K is that she wriggles her feet, whilst lying motionless on the couch, in an unconscious bid for freedom.

Another friend, who is a yoga teacher, had a different association, to an ancient form of yoga known as "Kundalini". It refers to a latent feminine energy believed to lie coiled at the base of the spine. Kundalini is a system of meditation directed towards the release of this energy. This is, of course, available to both men and women. Intensely spiritual and sensual, the movements arise in spirals from deep within the pelvis and emanate upwards throughout the rest of the body. Practitioners can experience ecstasy. I am reminded of the Christian religious mystics.

To come back to Earth, the balanced and unhampered description of the biologists of female anatomy can only serve to enhance better living, greater equality, and more tolerance. Education is essential in furthering society to be able to make the best gains from our world as it is presented to us.

CHAPTER TWO

The anatomy of the clitoris: a re-interpretation

I make no apology for beginning this chapter on anatomy from a psychoanalytic point of view since it is really the whole purpose of writing the book. The psychoanalyst Michael Parsons writes about there being a biological basis to our physical sexual beings. But he explains that it depends on how a particular society interprets what they find to determine how they understand it: "The nature of sexuality depends on how its irreducible biological basis is interpreted by a particular society at a particular time" (Parsons, 2000b, p. 37). He is referring to sexuality, but first, "irreducibility" does not allow for the evolutionary development from one species to another that will become relevant during this chapter. Theory follows a similar though speedier path, where change is at least demonstrable within a generation or two. Parsons uses the concept of a developmental stage and the way Klein changes it into a position as an important psychoanalytic example of what he is saying. What I find fascinating is that he is writing at a time when an important part of that biological basis, namely the structure of the clitoris, is actually being re-interpreted but he does not mention it, perhaps preferring not to draw attention to it.

Before that, in her ground-breaking book *The Gender Conundrum*, Dana Birksted-Breen states that "Anatomy is a given" (1993, p. 3). She goes on to describe that what each individual makes of this anatomy will influence the course of their own psychosexuality. Later in this book, I return again and again to Birksted-Breen's remarkable demonstration of the complexities of sexuality and her innovative conceptualisations to help to understand it (Chapters Three, Four, and Five). However, I do not think that the actual anatomy, or at least each generation of society's interpretation of it, has sufficient space for consideration; it is the main focus of this book. Before the millennium and not for the first time, albeit for different reasons, it is as if everything is so complex that at least one aspect, biology, can be taken as "given", so at least providing a starting point somewhere.

The above references to contemporary psychoanalytic writers bring Freud's classical statement right into the foreground of our consciousness:

> Biology is truly a land of unlimited possibilities ... and we cannot guess what answers it will return in a few dozen years to the questions we have put to it. They may be of a kind that will blow away the whole of our artificial structure of hypotheses.
>
> (Freud, 1920g, p. 60)

I am going to describe some scientific papers that appeared towards the end of the twentieth century, one in the Swedish gynaecological literature (Van Turnhout et al., 1995) and the other from Australia in the *Journal of Urology* (O'Connell et al., 1998). These papers put forward a re-interpretation of the anatomy of the clitoris. They see the structures traditionally labelled as the bulbs of the vestibule, which are situated around and internally above the small classical glans clitoris, as an integral part of the structure of the clitoris. Therefore, the clitoris is a much larger organ than previously thought.

These authors each published papers illustrating and describing a new interpretation of the structure of the clitoris involving the re-labelling of parts. However, the new understanding is itself still hidden within the stark language of science and still vulnerable to misunderstanding. "The cleft vulvar anatomy is homologue[1] to its non-cleft male counterpart" (Van Turnhout, 1995, p. 767). Immediately, it looks as if someone is saying that male and female are the same and the opportunity for further thinking is in ruins. The beauty of O'Connell's work is apparent in her anatomical drawings. Interestingly, the representations of internal female anatomy, particularly in the Van Turnhout paper, do look strangely male, only they are internal.

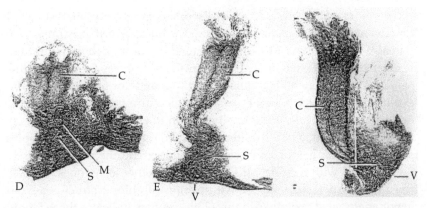

Figure 2. The female corpus spongiosum re-visited. Reprinted from *Acta Obstetricia Gynecologica Scandinavica*, Van Turnhout (1995). D: Toward the glans. The amount of spongious tissue (S) seems to diminish. Concentrations of the spongiosum are still to be found on both sides of the midline (M). The cavernosa (C) diminish in size while the septum is less pronounced. E: Just proximal to the glans cliioridis the corpora cavernosa (C) bend caudally. Their direction no longer paralleling the vestibular skin (V). This level shows the corpus spongiosum (S) only to be covered by vestibular epithelium. F: Ventral slide through the glans clitoridis. The glans ^ composed of spongious tissue (S), although the amount of vascular spaces is smaller than observed in the pars intermedia. The S^ms clitoridis has a hood-Tike appearance and covers the conjoined ends of both corpora cavernosa.

Attempting now to put this into a more descriptive form of language, the anatomical structure of the clitoris has been thought of until now as the small, even vestigial, glans clitoridis. What was being understood anew (and again, as will be apparent throughout this book) in the world of anatomical biology, leading to the re-labelling of the surrounding structures, is that the clitoris is not so small but that it has a similar structure to the penis. Both are made up of spongiose tissues that can expand in size on arousal, by filling with blood as we know happens in the male. Also, that the clitoris extends between and around the urethra and the vestibule of the vagina. It is as children imagine, a penis-equivalent, *hidden up inside*. These tissues were obviously always there before but they were named differently—as the bulbs of the vestibule—inside the entrance (introitus) to the vagina. In that way, they have had little or no significance for centuries of time past. O'Connell has renamed them as the bulbs of the clitoris.[2]

This information from another discipline caught my interest, and I saw the shift there as a parallel to how psychoanalytic theory on female sexuality had evolved in its passionate and stormy debate within the field and with others, namely the feminists, over the last century. In this new century, it is relatively quiet (I had to search for the new literature explored in Chapter Nine), but meanwhile more has happened in the urological press. Helen O'Connell went on to write other papers (2000, 2005a, 2005b, and 2008). I visited her in 2011, and she gave me copies of these papers. The first two validate and extend the original dissection findings with modern MRI imaging and other techniques. In 2000, she raises issues such as "Active deletion of clitoral structures from major anatomical textbooks in this (20th) century indicates the extent to which anatomy exists in a social framework" (Rees & O'Connell, 2000, p. 402). The third paper (and I ask my reader to remember that this is still being published in the *Journal of Urology*!) broadens this aspect and records what she had been talking about on her website. For instance, that there is a history of controversy and suppression surrounding the clitoris going back to the seventeenth century and forming a basis for the more recent coming to light of both medical and cultural practices of clitoridectomy (female genital mutlilation, FGM). She says, "for periods as long as 100 years anatomical knowledge of the clitoris appears to have been lost or hidden, presumably for cultural reasons" (O'Connell, 2005b, p. 1193). The final paper in 2008 acknowledges that there has been some controversy in her field and puts forward a revised new anatomical interpretation of the structures where several parts work together to achieve orgasm. These include the parts already brought together by her originally as the clitoris (1998), previously named the paired vestibular bulbs, the crura, and the bodies of the clitoris. They are internal structures and not the partially external glans, traditionally known as the clitoris. The focus of the paper is on the distal (lower third of) the vagina.

> The distal vagina is a structure that is so inter-related with the clitoris that it is a matter of some debate whether the two are truly separate structures. The same relationship applies to the female urethra.
>
> Also, the distal vagina, clitoris and urethra form an integrated entity ... These parts have a shared vasculature and nerve supply and during sexual stimulation respond as a unit though the responses are not uniform.
>
> (O'Connell, 2008, p. 1183)

How extraordinary to consider this when remembering the history of psychoanalytic theory of female sexuality, the debate about clitoral or vaginal orgasm. And then it was "resolved" by moving away from sex to motherhood!

The 2008 paper ends with:

> We recommend the naming of this tissue cluster or unified entity: *the clitoral complex*. The clitoral complex composed of the distal vagina, urethra, and clitoris, is the location of female sexual activity, analogous to the penis in men.
>
> (O'Connell, 2008, p. 1189)

This is all fascinating, but as I continued to think about it, I still felt there was a risk that it would keep coming back to "male and female are the same". Then I came across another biological author, this time in Italy, writing at the same time as the other interpretations in the *fin de siècle* years and opening up a little more space for thinking.

Toesca (1996), writing from Italy in the *Journal of Anatomy*, adds to the information provided by Turnhout in Sweden and O'Connell in Australia from another direction. She is examining the haemodynamic (venous flow of blood) events during sexual activity. The paper ends with a helpful summary:

> Thus, taking in mind the four haemodynamic events during the penile erection cycle (flaccidity, tumescence, rigidity, detumescence) (Tudoriu & Bourmer, 1983; Wespes & Schulman, 1986; Aboseif & Lue, 1988) and that the rigidity is due to the compression of the venous plexus, as described above, the absence of the venous plexus in the clitoris suggests that this organ achieves tumescence but not rigidity during sexual arousal. However, this aspect needs further investigation to establish whether the clitoris displays an erection cycle similar to that of the penis.
>
> (Toesca, 1996, p. 20)

So the male and female structures resemble each other much more closely than has been thought, but the female components are adapted for the part to be played. The idea, simultaneously romantic and anatomical, that the female accepts the male, is now cast in an interpretative culture that embraces more equality. While it endorses Dana Birksted-Breen's unconscious representational concept of "penis-as-link" (1996), at the same time that concept's name still does not quite capture the move within science and culture towards greater equality. Truly anticipating these discoveries at a psychological level, in name it still seems to me to be "too male".

The work of Masters and Johnson (1966) suggested that the clitoris has a role in conception. In addition, that it is structurally involved in childbirth. They had clarified photographically that the clitoris is continuous with the perivaginal[3] spongioform tissue. Though this was a turning point, and they had pre-empted the new anatomical labelling by thirty years, they did not emphasise this as a breakthrough. They were physiologists, more concerned with function than structure. They needed to avoid the feminist trap themselves at the time of being seen to be literally equating female with male. They were careful to say that whilst this makes the clitoris anatomically homologous with the penis, it does not make them exact complements. Their focus was then on the importance of female sexual response, which should be understood in itself. Arousal is both internal and external and involves the whole perineum perhaps sometime before tumescence of the clitoris. At a later stage, the plateau stage of orgasm, the clitoris retracts to provide the orgasmic platform in the female, offering support to the ejaculating penis.

Masters and Johnson were very explicit, but in my opinion, because of a mental disjunction in line with the age-old anxiety about sexual difference and sexual function, even though they state that "the clitoris retracts ...", it does not allow for the conceptualisation of the hidden parts of the clitoris that make up the receptive platform. Conceptually at the time, the platform was still made up of the clitoris *and* other, less inflammatory, more emotionally neutral parts of the female genitalia, "the vestibular bulbs, the crura ...". This anatomical discussion has even appeared in the psychoanalytic literature before, in a paper by Burton, "The meaning of perineal activity in women: an inner sphinx", published in the *Journal of the American Psychoanalytic Association* (1996). Using clinical material, she explores the unconscious fantasy of an inner, erotic, and powerful "organ". Though she acknowledges the size and parts of the clitoris, she still refers to the bulbs as being "vestibular" as if they are disconnected from the other parts of the clitoris (Burton, 1996, p. 243). Her reference is Brash (1953) in Cunningham's manual (1981)—the text we used in the Anatomy Long Room at medical school!

O'Connell's research, joining the structures to form a single entity, the clitoris as a whole, was to come thirty years after the work of Masters and Johnson and at the same time as, but in another discipline and on the other side of the world from, Burton.

The work of Masters and Johnson[4] was reported in the psychoanalytic literature by Sherfey (1966) and then also by Gillespie (1969). Gillespie records their findings, but later (1975) he is still concerned with female difficulty in achieving pleasure, the concern with frigidity first raised by Freud.[5] This concern also involves the controversy about clitoral as opposed to vaginal orgasm, and he goes back to anthropological evidence about the lower species. Gillespie had watched an Attenborough TV film that showed fish, male and female, expelling their sexual products into the same stretch of water with what *could* be interpreted as orgiastic wriggling. It is from the cloaca (the primitive common excretory cavity in birds, reptiles, and fish) that, in mammals and the human female, the vagina and uterus developed, separate from the main excretory channels, excretory now only of menstrual blood. His hypothesis is (drawn from Kemper, 1965) that whilst phylogenetically the male animal has preserved his way of sexual life through his development into a land animal, the female has been required by the process of evolution to develop a vagina and a uterus out of her cloaca. She has had to give up the pleasure that her "fish-ancestress" shared with her male partner in the service of internal impregnation. He suggests that "the human female, in our day at least, has learned again how to have an orgasm with the aid of just those muscle groups that go into action during male orgasm" (Gillespie, 1975, p. 7). Arising from this is the possibility that:

> woman's dissatisfaction with her role is rooted a great deal more deeply than mere envy of the male's possession of imposing external genitalia ... (women) are demanding to be liberated from that unfair share in the reproductive process which evolution has imposed on the female of the viviparous species.
>
> (Gillespie, 1975, p. 7)

This is a process that is still ongoing today. Melanie Klein offers a formulation for "frigidity, occurring in different degrees" in a number of cases she treated, "a result of unstable attitudes to the penis, based mainly on a flight from the primal object. The capacity for full oral gratification, which is rooted in a satisfactory relation to the mother, is the basis for experiencing full genital orgasm (Freud)" (Klein, 1975, p. 200).

These ideas illustrate that none of this is new. But they do illustrate just how difficult it has been at the socio-cultural level, for a secure means of reproduction to evolve and for a space for a baby to be visualised, while also maintaining an organ of female sexual enjoyment. This is illustrated in its extreme in the unconscious envy of sexual pleasure for young women by older women in the cultures that practise female circumcision. The influence of the cloaca persists, and sex is often viewed as messy or dirty, and much dirtier for women (see Perelberg, 2015). Young girls still deal with these difficulties by being sexually anaesthetised, frigid.

Sherfey (1966) had suggested a revision of the Freudian theory that had demanded an impossible separation between clitoral and vaginal orgasm, but also highlighted Masters and Johnson's finding of the capacity of the female for multiple orgasms, each creating more tension, … saying that it is "only culture that restricts her behaviour" (quoted in Birksted-Breen, 1993, p. 12).

Montgrain is another psychoanalytic author who strays bravely into the biological world. He considers further the difficult path from anatomical destiny to psychic representation in the girl. He speaks of Freud's irremediable consequences ascribed to the discrepancy in size between penis and visible clitoris and the secretiveness about the latter, but then acknowledges "excitement and sexual sensations that are invasive but lack precise contours and for which she has no mental representation" (Montgrain, 1983, p. 170). Freud's "irremediable consequences" refers to his view that female sexuality becomes closed in terms of development at a relatively early age. His contention, which would not hold weight today, is that:

> A man of about thirty strikes us as a youthful, somewhat unformed individual, whom we expect to make powerful use of the possibilities for development opened up to him by analysis. A woman of the same age, however, often frightens us by her psychical rigidity and unchangeability.
>
> (Freud, 1933a, p. 143)

Montgrain notes that "the interesting revelations of Masters and Johnson have not yet completely erased all the old prejudices" (1983, p. 169). He comments that the actual frequency of feminine frigidity resulting from social and moral controls and repression tends to underestimate the intensity and overflowing capacity of women's sexuality.

The different generations of biological work carried out in the mid-twentieth century and then at the millennium must inform psychoanalytic theory, and I have referred to some authors who have tried to do this before. They offer us the chance to resolve some of the conflicts and prejudices in the psychoanalytic theory of female sexuality hotly debated until now (see Chapter Three). It concerns not only anatomy but, more importantly, function. It has implications for female pleasure, that forbidden entity which has been historically under male control, as explored in Chapter One. It provides an evolutionary pathway for motherhood and feminine identification. This controversial biological evidence supports the fact that because of the inaccurate labelling of parts, it has been overlooked or misunderstood that the actual structure of the clitoris incorporates the musculature surrounding the vagina, making clitoral and vaginal orgasm aspects of the same myriad of female experience, lifted out of the physical by Lacan in his concept of jouissance.

No longer can vagina and clitoris be thought to be separate, with completely different functions and situated at an unhelpful distance from each other. This was an almost derogatory belief held previously, implying all the things that women are vulnerable to criticism about, women (their erotic life)—partly owing to the stunting effect of civilized conditions and partly owing to their conventional secretiveness and insincerity—is still veiled in an impenetrable obscurity (Freud, 1905, p. 151). The clitoris encircles the lower third of the vagina and is not purely for pleasure. The anatomical insights convey that the clitoris also supports and is involved in the structures concerned with conception and childbearing; that being a woman is an integrated, substantial, and genuine entity.

Historical note

For me, it is a fascinating thing to do, to dip into a textbook like *Gray's Anatomy* again, after many years since doing the same as a medical student and a junior doctor undergoing basic surgical training. I felt it was necessary while preparing this book, to catch a personal glimpse of what the modern-day surgeons (the urologists and gynaecologists I have quoted) were concerned about. New editions of *Gray's Anatomy* have been published about every five to ten years since the original edition in 1858, until the forty-first edition in 2015. The Wellcome Museum Library, an historical collection, holds a random selection of its editions from the twentieth century. These show that the statement in the Swedish paper of 1995, "The cleft vulvar anatomy is homologue to its non-cleft male counterpart", takes the word "homologue" from the entry concerning the anatomy of the clitoris from *Gray's Anatomy*, persistent over time: "The clitoris is an erectile structure homologous to the penis …". It goes on to describe two corpora cavernosa making up the body of the clitoris. However, an authentic re-edition of the fifteenth edition has the word "analogous". "The clitoris is an erectile structure analogous to the corpora cavernosa of the penis" (Gray, 1901, p. 1009). It is interesting to speculate on this change of word, after which time O'Connell says that more detailed drawings were removed. How different in meaning are these two words? It probably warrants a discussion. But a new word is introduced, only being discussed in the literature nearly one hundred years later. The original word reappeared but the drawings did not.

Meanwhile, the drawings throughout the last century illustrate only the partially external glans clitoridis. But in the 1901 edition, an attempt to show the internal parts of the clitoris as a labelled schematic band, dissected out from the lower third of the vagina, is clearly different and more illustrative of the hidden parts of the clitoris (Gray, 1901, pp. 1008–1013). As O'Connell noted, this detail disappeared from later editions. The chapter is headed "Organs of generation" and lists the female organs—uterus, ovaries, etc. … mammary glands. "The bulbs of the vestibule" (renamed more recently by O'Connell as the "bulbs of the clitoris") are listed, but separately and at a distance in the list from the clitoris. The figure that appears in all the subsequent editions shows the glans clitoridis only in a direct and rather disturbing diagram of the external female genitalia surrounding a gaping introitus. It is enough just to ask the reader to imagine Edvard Munch's painting *The Scream*, and to ponder on the associations to this.

Other than these changes more than a century ago, not much in the text or the diagrams (in this small section on the clitoris) seems to change, though the general format of the book as a whole becomes modern and colourful more recently. There are references to the clitoris being a smaller version of the penis but different from it in being separate from the urethra.

I have tried not to focus on this issue of size too much throughout my book, since it has handicapped the development of theory so much over the century of psychoanalysis. But it seems to me that the capacity of the cervix and the vagina to expand during childbirth is an issue of real importance developmentally. This anatomical evolution underpins the change of focus from the first theory of female sexuality of Freud, about penis envy and castration anxiety, to the second, promoted by Jones, about the capacity to have a baby. The structure of the internal parts of the clitoris, thought by some to include the bulbs of the vestibule, becomes lost in the controversy. The truth is that there is more similarity in structure between male and female than has been generally understood, though with obvious differences. Examples are the partial relation of the clitoris to the urethra and the "cleftness" (divided in two) of some of the structures in the female. The discrepancy in size and its significance has been exaggerated unhelpfully and to deal with anxiety. It is not just in the world of psychoanalysis that controversy impacts on the development of theory so that it might take more than a century to resolve; it seems to be in the complex nature of sexual difference itself. This, to me, seems to be directly expressed by Freud's later theory of female sexuality, the repudiation of femininity.

The historical development of the psychoanalytic theory of female sexuality (1897–2000)*

Because the psychoanalytic literature on female sexuality is so vast, this review can be only an ideosyncratic tour of it. My focus is to convey how it falls into a passionate debate but with a repeating pattern, circular and concentric, almost mirroring the structure of the female anatomy itself. Developments in theory in America and France departed from each other in very different directions, and Dana Birksted-Breen summarises this succinctly in a new introduction to psychoanalysis edited by Budd and Rusbridger (2005). She emphasises an important collection in France by Chasseguet-Smirgel (1964) that followed Klein and then Lacan, who underlined Freud's wish to leave biology aside and developed the theory of the phallus.

My starting point is an American book that provides a comprehensive list[1] of the literature throughout the twentieth century until its date of publication in 1991 (Schuker & Levinson, *Female Psychology: An Annotated Bibliography*, Chapter 18 on "Sexuality"). To try to make sense of the history, I compiled a grid (Figure 3), adding relevant references from 1991 until 2000.

---

*For the years since 2000, see Chapter Nine.

Date	Author	Title or concept	Comment or historical link
1905	**Freud**	*Three Essays on the Theory of Sexuality*	Theoretical and clinical basis of later theories of female sexuality and character development
1915		*On narcissism*	Penis envy Castration complex applied to:
1925		*Some psychical consequences of the anatomical distinction between the sexes*	Female sexuality
1931		*Female sexuality*	
1933		*Femininity*	
1920	**Abraham**	Wish fulfilment and revengeful penis envy	1943 **Hayward**
1924	**Horney**	Female castration complex Primary and secondary	
1927		Penis envy v. feminine genital anxiety	1996 **Dorsey** "concept of feminine genital anxiety ... lost in a sea of literature", p. 286
1932	**Klein**	Dominant feminine instinctual disposition. Penis envy secondary to oral envy of maternal breast and the mother's body and contents	

Year	Author		
1933	**Jones**	(Innate primary femininity) "the earliest stage of their development is essentially feminine", p. 31	1968 **Stoller** term first coined within framework of gender identity
			1997 **Elise** erroneous if used as if it is a unitary concept; **Kulish** review (2000)
1937	**Jacobson**	Superego formation and female castration complex Greater female self-esteem and autonomy Fear of vaginal injury rather than fear of loss of love object	
1943	**Hayward**	Two types of female castration reaction Revengeful (pre-oedipal) Wish fulfilment (oedipal) "women who orientate their lives around penis envy"	1920 **Abraham**
1964	**Grunberger**	Intrication (complex entanglement) of oral, anal, and vaginal schemata Clitoris only organ purely for pleasure	
1966	**Masters and Johnson**	Orgasm produced by clitoral stimulation, direct or <u>indirect</u>	1933 **Freud** re-examination of hypothesis that women must evolve from clitoral to vaginal orgasm as development proceeds

BIOLOGICAL/PHYSIOLOGICAL

27

(Continued)

Figure 3 (Continued)

Date	Author	Title or concept	Comment or historical link
1968	**Kestenberg**	Inner and outer genitality	
1968	**Stoller**	Primary femininity	
1969	**Gillespie**	Concepts of vaginal orgasm	1933 **Freud** 1966 **Masters and Johnson**
1970	**Montrelay**	Phallocentrism and concentricity	
1972	**Stoller**	Power of influence of psychological forces in opposition to biological state	
1973	**Lacan**	Jouissance	"Phallic" re "nothing"/space
1974	**Abrams and Shengold**	The meaning of nothing	1993 **Kalinich**
1975	**Gillespie**	Evolutionary schema	
1976	**Chasseguet-Smirgel**	The "dark continent"	1926 **Freud**
1977	**Eissler**	Comments on penis envy and orgasm in women INTERDISCIPLINARY	
1980	**Chiland**	Relation of clinical practice to theory	Freud's inhibition in identifying with a woman

Year	Author	Topic	Notes
1982	**Kestenberg**	Early maternal or inner genital phase	The role theory may play in obscuring rather than clarifying clinical data
1984	**De Goldstein**	Clitoris not subject to detumescence	
1991	**Kulish**	*Mental representation of the clitoris: the fear of female sexuality*	1966 **Masters & Johnston**
1991	**SCHUKER AND LEVINSON**	FEMALE PSYCHOLOGY: AN ANNOTATED BIBLIOGRAPHY. CHAP 18: SEXUALITY	Leaves out **Lacan** (1972) Passing reference to work about him in other sections
1992	**Richards**	Sphincter control and genital sensation	
1993	**Kalinich**	Sense of absence	
1995	**Van Turnout**	Restructuring the clitoris BIOLOGICAL	
1996	**Birksted-Breen**	*Unconscious representation of femininity*	
1996	**Burton**	Penis-as-link	
1996		The meaning of perineal activity	Unconscious fantasy of an inner, erotic, and powerful "organ"
1996	**Dorsey**	Feminine genital anxiety	1926 **Horney**
1996	**Richards**	Primary femininity and female genital anxiety	Link to urinary musculature

(Continued)

29

Figure 3 (Continued)

Date	Author	Title or concept	Comment or historical link
1997	**Melnick**	Metaphor in developmental stages	
1997	**Elise**	Primary sense of femaleness	
1998	**Gilmore**	Cloacal anxiety	
1998	**O'Connell**	Restructuring of the clitoris BIOLOGICAL	
2000	**Kulish**	Primary femininity REVIEW	1997 **Elise** Primary sense of femaleness
2001	**Balsam**	Maternality	

Figure 3. The historical development of the psychoanalytic theory of female sexuality shown as a grid. Compiled from Schuker and Levinson (1991), *Female Psychology: An Annotated Bibliography*, chapter 18: Sexuality. Penryn: The Atlantic Press.

The grid shows clearly the pattern I have described. The fourth column shows some of the gyrations over time, how theorists lose and then sometimes come back to terms previously coined. In each era, new theories are presented, but they tend to be received with a passionately inflamed controversy and then they disappear. Decades later, they re-emerge.[2] This mirrors the history of the development of knowledge of the female in other disciplines over history, governed by social and cultural mores and then suppressed. In this parallel way, the drawings of the female sexual organs disappeared from the anatomy books in the Middle Ages and again from *Gray's Anatomy* at the beginning of the twentieth century (see Chapters One and Two).

Looking at the grid, there are the classic views of Freud, Klein, and Jones and the women who first challenged Freud, like Horney and Deutsch. (Dinora Pines took this line of thought into the next generation.) Freud conceptualised male sexual development but found that the female did not fit in. This gives rise to the faulty concept of female sexuality being, of itself, "pathological". (Here is a clue to the vehemence that can often fuel the response to any writing.) The differences between the early theories became formalised into the dual theory response, or the "Freud–Jones" debate. Freud regarded the clitoris as the leading erotogenic zone in the female and believed that this had to change to the vagina in puberty in order for the woman to achieve true femininity. In Jones' theory of female sexuality, drawing more on the Kleinian notion of early knowledge of the vagina and the womb and the prominence of motherhood, there was an attempt to bridge the gap from an emotional point of view.

In fact, Klein hugely redressed "the penis/vagina imbalance" (personal communication, Jane Milton). She took forward Abraham's ideas about the early knowledge of the vagina. But in her vast writings, Klein did not usually name the vagina and the clitoris, preferring instead to use "the female genital", perhaps adding to the separation from anatomical accuracy. Jones' ideas on female sexuality stemmed very much from Klein's, both moving psychoanalysis inwards to concentrate on "interiority".

This early classical work was followed by a rich tapestry of more modern theories, each subjected to the same fiery response, whether it be Lacanian jouissance (1972); or "concentricity" (Grunberger, 1964; Montrelay, 1970); the desire to penetrate versus the desire to be penetrated, a metaphorisation of bodily experience (Cosnier 1987; Gibeault, 1988);

penis desire as opposed to envy (Gillespie, 1975); primary femininity (Kulish 1991; Stoller, 1968); or cloacal anxiety (Gilmore, 1998); and many others, all at risk of reductionism or looseness. (This paragraph is necessarily condensed here but is expanded upon in Chapter Four.) Further examples of the familiar pattern emerged, coloured by the international differences, whether the literature came from the UK, following on from the original classical theories; or a more philosophical approach coming from France; and the modern American literature enlarged extensively on the issues of motherhood and feminine identification.

To illustrate this pattern, I recently came across a paper by Margaret Arden (1987), revisiting a paper, "A concept of femininity", by Sylvia Payne (1935). Arden picks up on Marjorie Brierley's notion of a psychological definition of femininity as "integration". They are focusing on the quality of feminine thinking as integrative. Of course, feminine thinking can be done by female or male (see Chapter Five), but to me this connects to the embodiment of that thinking within the structure of the female anatomy as conceptualised in Chapter Two. It seems to anticipate and embrace both the concentric, internalised structures of the female body represented in the mind and the function of motherhood. Even though Jones supported these views coming from female writers at the time of the Freud–Jones debate (in keeping with the times, a debate that could not be had directly by the women), the extent of these ideas might now be thought to belong to a much later era. The dynamic of the feminine being hidden and secret applies to what can happen to the very literature itself.

Kulish does takes up this quality of the literature itself, saying that there are theoretical gyrations around the idea of "primary femininity" (Kulish, 2000, p. 1363). This concept serves to illustrate further some of the characteristics the theoretical writing and discussion take on, probably already apparent in my writing, which in turn emulates the subject matter. Kulish agrees with Elise (1997) that the concept of primary femininity brought important advances in understanding the psychology of women as well as accompanying contradictions and problematic assumptions. Elise argued that the term "primary femininity" imparts the erroneous idea that femininity is primary, derived in a pre-ordained way from the female body. She expresses caution in this field, suggesting that when considering female development it is easy to fall into "a quicksand of assumptions" (p. 496). She proposed that we use the phrase "primary sense of femaleness". It would shift the focus in the right direction—towards studying the multiple influences on the little girl's development, of a positive sense of being female, and thus diminishing misleading and faulty conceptual ties (Elise, 1997, p. 500).

But Kulish feels that the problems with the concept extend further than Elise took them. "Primary femininity" has not been confined to studies of gender identity or the "primary sense of femaleness" but has appeared in numerous other contexts and frames of reference. This leads to more clinical and theoretical dilemmas. To look more easily at this problem was why I initially found myself drawing up the grid (Figure 3). At this point, I also tried to list the various frames of reference (Figure 4).

Figure 4. Some frames of reference used in the psychoanalytic theory of female sexuality.

Another example of the "gyrations" is seen in Dorsey (1996) and the concept of "feminine genital anxiety". It was first described by Horney in 1926 and was then "lost in a sea of literature" until Dorsey revived it in 1996.

Some biological imagery was introduced in Chapter Two. Here is an example of how it translates into psychoanalytic theory. Kulish, in "The mental representation of the clitoris: the fear of female sexuality", gives clinical material distinguishing between male and female psyche at orgasm. Whilst a man describes *spasms*, a woman will call it *spinning* (Kulish, 1991, pp. 522–523). This is most important when we come later to the concept of concentricity within the psychoanalytic sphere. But for the moment, if we study the grid, the theory, of itself, spins through the twentieth century with a concentricity of its own. I could imagine a grid in three dimensions might represent this in spiral form more vividly.

All these theories and images sit in overlapping parallel with the central backbone of psychoanalysis; for example, the unconscious, the Oedipus complex, castration anxiety, and bisexuality. They are presented as theories of mind but are equally illustrative of the body. Arden's comment about the awareness of Payne and Brierley's "integrative aspect of feminine thinking" was that it "is a landmark in the development of holistic thinking about psychoanalysis" (Arden, 1987, p. 239). In *The Dove that Returns, the Dove that Vanishes*, Parson's description of Freud's conception of the Oedipus complex is helpful here because he illuminates for us that Freud never defined it as a precise theory. Instead, he says the Oedipus complex pervades Freud's thinking throughout his work as if it were a subject the writing of which makes elusive (Parsons, 2000a, pp. 105–114). I think this applies even more so to the theory of female sexuality, already underlined by Birksted-Breen (1993).

So, as Parker (1986) states:

> the body never stops haunting the presumed anatomy of the unconscious, never stops littering the field of psychoanalysis .... Anatomy, then, is neither fully destiny nor lack of destiny in its psychoanalytic conceptuality: it is instead what might be termed it's a-destiny, that which prevents psychoanalysis from completely coming into its own as Theory, from thinking that it escapes the body when it defines itself against it.
>
> (in Birksted-Breen, 1993, p. 21)

Again, Freud can be heard warning us:

> I object to all of you to the extent that you do not distinguish more
> clearly between what is psychic and what is biological, that you try
> to establish a neat parallelism between the two … we must try to
> keep psychoanalysis separate from biology just as we have kept it
> separate from anatomy and physiology.
>
> (Freud, 1935, unpublished letter, in Young-Bruehl, 1990, p. 349)

There is a fine line between separating from these realities completely and concretising their influence only to lose sight of the psychoanalytic.

It is my belief that the conceptualisation of how the anatomy is interpreted at a physical level is essential before a modern psychoanalytic theory, so wished for and needed in the field of female sexuality, can be established. But what is extraordinary, and evidence of the power of the unconscious, is that throughout attempts to formulate the psychoanalytic theory of female sexuality over more than a century, the "littering" that Parker describes actually allows the theory, via the unconscious, to anticipate the modern physical interpretation. This is of a clitoris made up of various other structures previously labelled separately (see Chapter Two). This interpretation works to integrate the theories in a more comprehensive way, as male and female anatomy can be seen as more balanced in relation to each other. There is the penis and then there is the vagina, encircled by a clitoris resembling the penis in structure and sexual function, but belonging to the childbearing structures. Remember that O'Connell (2008) has even concluded that it is so intimately connected to the urethra as well that it cannot really be considered as a separate organ. So even like the penis, its musculature must play a part in the urinary excretory system. This together with the distal vagina, so that, with this anatomical interpretation, no longer can the vagina and the clitoris in psychoanalytic theory be thought to be separate structures at an unhelpful distance from each other.

Lastly, I have already, in Chapter Two, discussed a psychoanalytic paper by Anna Burton (1996) when focusing on the anatomy. Burton describes the anatomy, as seen later by O'Connell, in a very similar way, linking the other structures, the crura, the vestibular bulbs, the clitoral bodies, to the external glans clitoris. But she does not go as far as O'Connell does, to say that these are an integral part of the clitoris.

Her source is Brash (1953), quoted in *Cunningham's Textbook of Anatomy*. Here is a prime example of psychoanalysis incorporating, anticipating future insights but in the nature of the hidden subject matter itself, as I have described, not finding a way for a sustainable change in understanding.

Part II

CHAPTER FOUR

The anatomy of the clitoris: clinical evidence of psychic representation

Introduction

The conscious difficulty for the little girl is in knowing how things are structured on the inside. She looks at a boy (as he does simultaneously) and sees exactly how it is, how the penis wees, becomes erect, how it is so seemingly different from her own make-up. Freud has documented in detail what both children, girl and boy, universally make of this. McDougall summarises it: "other women don't have a penis but my mother does … or did, but father took it away … or else it's *hidden up inside her*" (McDougall, 1972, p. 379; my italics). In this way, the fantasies of children provide a clue to the hidden reality until now buried under the universal fear and prejudice in adults that develops out of childhood anxieties about castration. Of course, it is not a penis hidden up inside her but the evolutionarily developed equivalent, the clitoris. Instead of two functional systems, the dual one for the excretion of urine and the emission of semen and the bowel and anus for the excretion of faeces, there are three systems for the woman, the third created to make a space for a baby. But these three biological systems are hidden and not numbered. Because they are so intimately arranged in relation to each other, the little girl can grow up to think that it is all part of the same, that everything happens in a primitive cloacal space from which, in fact, evolution has released her. The only evidence of the similarity to the male is in the tiny "vestigial clitoris" visible on exploration and being so small, vulnerable to all the second-class-status heaped upon women over the centuries. Together with the cloacal mess, this adds up to Perelberg's "Abject" so directly, with the shame, inferiority, dirtiness, evil, and control by the power of men it conjures up. Kristeva's idea is emphasised, that where there is maternal breakdown, there is a collapse of the paternal laws (Perelberg, 2015, p. 169).

The girl who is brought up positively, to identify with the mother and the mother's pregnant body (Balsam, 1996), comes to understand a little more than this about herself unconsciously as she develops. Instead, there is an un-thought awareness of the way the body functions that incorporates the idea of a much larger and muscular clitoris, similar though not identical in structure to the penis and internal rather than external to the body. It surrounds the vagina, helping to support its functions of the passage of monthly menstruation out, or of semen in, and when conception has occurred, the transport of a baby. It has a role in both conception and in childbirth therefore. Traditionally thought to have only the role of achieving orgasm, in fact it brings together vaginal and clitoral orgasm, so hotly debated in psychoanalytic theory, as the same thing, or perhaps versions of the same thing since orgasm can be varied and multiple. In a fascinating way, though, much of the psychoanalytic theory on the subject throughout the twentieth century seems to reach out in anticipation of the modern biological interpretation of the female structures that lifts this inequality between the sexes out of its anthropological past.

But among the most passionate of psychoanalytic endeavours is a commitment to classical theory and its development along scientifically agreed lines. Included in this is a specific focus on the internal world of the mind that is monitored very closely, should it broaden to include too much about the body. Human sexuality is particularly controversial in this regard, and Kohon, drawing on Freud, states in his essay on hysteria that, "From a psychoanalytic point of view it is not possible to appeal to biology to explain the difference between the sexes" (Kohon, 1999, p. 10). It is not surprising, therefore, that this kind of information from other disciplines can present a problem if it seems to question established theory too directly.

Along these lines, in *The Gender Conundrum* (1993), Birksted-Breen reminds us that it is the psychological representation of the body that is crucial for psychoanalysis. But Freud wrote in 1920 that "Biology is truly a land of unlimited possibilities ... and we cannot guess what answers it will return in a few dozen years to the questions we have put to it. They may be of a kind that will blow away the whole of our artificial structure of hypotheses" (Freud, 1920g, p. 60). Medical science has indeed moved on, so we have to be clear about the psychological representation of the body as it is understood now in the twenty-first century. Freud at different times argued for biology and against biology. We live in a phase of development of theory in which it seems to have gone entirely one way.

When examining change in general, the threat to the *status quo* gives rise to considerable anxiety. Psychoanalytic theory is no exception, and it is understandable to look for some "givens" in order to begin to address change. The physical body that we see is a natural example. Birksted-Breen, in her Introduction, states that "Anatomy is a given" (1993, p. 3). It is as if something has to be thought of as fixed in order to contemplate the shifting complexities of everything else. Parsons opens this up when he refers to "how the irreducible biological basis is interpreted by a particular society at a particular time" (Parsons, 2000b, p. 37) in order to examine change to psychoanalytic theory along socio-cultural lines. Knowledge and understanding about the body too can change, and this must affect its psychic representation in our minds.

This chapter will keep in mind the changes in the anatomical labelling of the female form in the biological world and examine some of the consequences for psychoanalytic theory in the area of ideas such as penis envy and castration anxiety, to try to cast some more light on Freud's "dark continent".

I will present a patient who came to analysis with dissociation and confusion about her sexuality that began to resolve as a result of the analysis. She is a young adult woman who, as a solution to her emotional difficulties, has determined to live life without sex. Her renunciation suggests an intense unconscious curiosity about what is inside her that was apparent from the beginning of the analysis and expressed itself strongly in the transference.

This example addresses the impact of the evolution of the cloaca on unconscious representations in women. The patient described experiences in childhood of feeling poisoned by her mother's venomous control and of an uncle's perversion, so that she is left with an undeveloped or perverted representation of her genitalia as an undefined mess of poison and rubbish. Unable to express her rage, this too comes out in violent dreams. But as Gilmore (1998), who writes about cloacal anxiety, says of her own patient, Ms T:

> Again, this patient's concerns and anxieties are far more complex than any singular conceptualisation can encompass; she struggles with a mixture of bodily anxieties, narcissistic concerns, interpersonal urges and inhibitions and conflicts around aggression and sexuality.
>
> (Gilmore, 1998, p. 463)

Clinical material 1

Miss K[1] was in her early twenties. She was pretty and vivacious, and, by her own accounts, tantalised her male friends. Whilst she adhered to her resolution to live without sex, she could be carefree. This led to a problem during the sessions because the taboo extended to the actual words that might describe her problem. For many months, she edited and censored her speech, unable to utter words such as "sex" or "penis". Yet it was in her motivation to come to analysis at all that this was what she was preoccupied by and needing to focus on all the time, and she kept referring indirectly to it. This gave rise to an atmosphere highly charged with anxiety, fear, and excitement, enormously frustrating and titillating, and leaving me thinking about hysteria but also perversity.

Her carefree façade was maintained against a rigid and torturing internal framework that prohibited all adult pleasures whilst demanding her role to be that of a slave to the whims of others; her mother, with whom she still lived; her employer, in a menial part-time job; and now her analyst. But this presentation of herself as a lonely victim was flawed and masked a defiance. She had telephoned her mother regularly whilst away at university, saying that she was about to go off to bed, but then deceiving her and going out clubbing with her friends.

Her father had disappeared when she was aged four. He re-emerged after an acrimonious divorce, with a new family, and the patient had some contact with them against a backdrop of her mother's displeasure. Her conflict was extreme, and she hated both her father and her stepmother in order to remain unconscious of her hatred for her mother.

For a long time, the only expression of the darker side to Miss K was in her dreams, or nightmares as she called them. Unlike the difficulty about sex, although she was in deep conflict about telling me their content, she did so with what appeared to be a salacious plea-sure. They ranged from: the wrong heads (animal) on the wrong bodies (human); or large heads on small bodies; to a man trying to pull her under water to drown her; a man battering her with a hammer; to a recurrent dream about evil people trying to murder her and then eating her whilst she was still alive. The violence suggested to me that she had experienced abuse.

Meanwhile, she lay motionless on the couch, like a marble effigy on a mausoleum. The only movement would be a sudden rhythmical wriggling of the toes in rebellious protest against something I had said, usually about her relationship to her mother or to me, sometimes about her struggle to become an adult and sexual female. To me, it was as if her feet expressed the anxiety displaced from her genitals. It looked sexual, like an orgiastic discharge. Later, she began to shake her head vigorously as well, as if the capacity to maintain her two-dimensional and blinkered existence was increasingly threatened. But belying her innocence, when she arrived for her sessions she would consistently and coquettishly, though probably unconsciously, lift a corner of her long cardigan as she lay down as if showing me her knickers.

In the following excerpt from a Monday session soon after she had managed to move away from her mother's house, a dynamic shift appeared to take place. The atmosphere was charged with *expectancy*. Characteristically, the patient seemed to be waiting for me to ask. Even-tually, she made a few disjointed and tantalising references to her new flat and then remembered a time when she was still at school. Instead of carrying out her mother's wishes for the evenings that week, she had deceived her and claimed to be in the school play. She told me that she had only really been behind the scenes but, even there, she had "got into trouble". She *laboured* this point, telling me in several differ-ent ways about the consequences. Linking it to the words in my own countertransference response, I found myself taking up her expression *got into trouble* as a euphemism for getting *pregnant*. Triumphantly, she responded, "There couldn't be a pregnancy because I could never get near enough to a man to have sex, I couldn't."

I was aware that I was in the mother's position, deceived and carry-ing the burden of worrying about her vulnerability. In my chronic state of frustration, forgetting for a moment that I was an analyst and pro-pelled back to a position in, say, the family planning clinic, I could not contain a pointed remark of enactment. Almost under my breath I said,

"That's what they all say". She resisted this strongly so that I continued the analogy, saying she wanted to *abort* an idea that seemed to
have been created between us. There was further resistance to the idea
that it can be more likely to get pregnant the more the possibility is
denied. Then she said, "Well, it's not going to happen to me ..." (her
tone changed and a sparkle appeared in her voice) "unless someone
forces me, that is".

This confirming my worries, I said that I felt she was always trying to get me to force her to say things. Reflecting on the session afterwards, I felt amazed by the conversation we had been able to have in
that she had allowed herself to say the actual words, like "sex" and
"pregnancy".

After this confrontation between us, she could at least speak more
freely and the sexual words necessary to describe her worries were no
longer censored. It emerged that during her childhood an uncle had
exposed her to his wild transvestite parties when left to babysit and had
once exposed himself to her by demonstrating his ability to look like a
woman sexually, by tucking his penis between his legs. He had contributed further to her "sex education" by telling her that babies often died
in utero because women's insides were rotten and disgusting.

Her mother, meanwhile, had a series of boyfriends who were
invited home. In the child's understanding, they could be heard "beat-
ing up" her mother. Miss K would lie in bed terrified by the mother's
screams. She imagined the man to be raping her mother, treating her
like a piece of meat, as was now repeated in her dreams. So she had
determined to live her own life fulfilled in every way but without sex.
Her main aim had become to move away from her mother. A healthy
aim in theory, but she did it in such a way as to put the analysis and
herself at risk. She chose a flat that made things impractical geographi-
cally, and she had moved in with several unknown, single young men.
Now she was with strangers, I feared for her safety. I felt left with the
worry about her naivety and vulnerability.

After moving house and the dramatic shift that had occurred in the
language we could use, it was not long before Miss K met a young
man (not one of her new flatmates), with whom a relationship began to
develop. Characteristically, she did not tell me about any sexual contact,
but a particular trauma occurred at about this time that seemed to sym-
bolise her anxieties. Her car was broken into and everything stolen—
money, credit cards, and filofax. She missed a session over the car and

then missed more sessions as urgent doctors' appointments became the excuse. There was still an atmosphere of vulnerability to risk and the combination of the boyfriend, the violent penetration of her car, and the visits to the doctor continued to leave me with the anxious preoccupation about pregnancy. In reality, the doctor was needed because she had "honeymoon" cystitis, and she presented this in dramatic, traumatised detail on her return. But the relationship continued to develop and then she found a full-time professional job, ending her analysis for "practical reasons" shortly afterwards.

I am using Miss K's material here to illustrate how anxieties about her sexual status and development could be projected into me and processed from that distance until she was ready to own the implications herself. Her unconscious fear was of penetration, into the undefined mess of her "cloaca", and the turning point came when I said something very penetrating to her. But she must have felt safe, comforted, able to begin to identify with someone who could be realistic and more structured about sexuality. Someone who could feed back to her the tantalisation and frustration she induced in her objects, whilst she worked through the perverse, confusing, and traumatic roots of her self-discovery, to come to terms with both positive and negative aspects of her aggression.

Complementarity and concentricity

It is interesting to note that the literature on female sexuality throughout the twentieth century has a quality of circularity, new authors always returning to the same questions and concepts (Figure 3). The language and understanding of psychoanalysis predates the recent anatomical findings in exploring the mind and how the body is represented there. It is exciting now to be able to verify where originally it was almost right about the body but misunderstood through mis-labelling, as Freud predicted, and where it has been moving towards greater accuracy in concepts I will presently focus upon. But there is still a risk of being misunderstood now. The challenge is in saying that male and female are much more similar anatomically than we have wanted to think without being misunderstood to be saying that male and female are the same. The issue is about complementarity, which does not mean total symmetry of shape and function, or a reason to name a female organ, the clitoris, as a penis and therefore male. It is the accurate labelling of the *parts* of the female organ, according to the anatomical similarities with the male, that can subtly shift the meaning of psychoanalytic theory and synchronise previously diverse theories.

Birksted-Breen begins from the duality in Freud's theory of sexuality—biological or psychological destiny. She describes a disjunction between them, later called an out-of-focusness, creating a tension that is greater in relation to women, and she believes that this has fuelled the long debate about female sexuality. It gives rise to an opposition in the unconscious of a femininity represented as a lack and a femininity that is represented more as a space with "concentric" aspects (Birksted-Breen, 1993, pp. 1–37).

Her ideas particularly recognise French psychoanalytic contributions that have introduced greater complexities, such as the concept of "concentricity". This holds that the woman's body and its representation in her unconscious is arranged concentrically—rather like Russian dolls—organs (and the baby) within organs (Grunberger, 1964; Montrelay, 1970), and psychologically, developmental levels within other developmental levels (Melnick, 1977). This moves us towards a more accurate three-dimensional construction of the female make-up. Grunberger describes "the intrication [by which is meant the complex entanglement] of archaic, oral, anal and vaginal schemata" (*Recherches*, 1964, p. 103).[2] Birksted-Breen acknowledges that "Grunberger analyses feminine narcissism", that which characterises "the libidinal cathexis of the woman, is it's concentric character *and* at the same time the phallus" (*Recherches*, p. 103). Montrelay, in her structuring of the feminine unconscious as a play of forces, suggests that phallocentrism and concentricity appear firstly and more spectacularly as anxiety, and, inversely, in sublimation, and that "each of these determining processes of the unconscious economy will be seen at play in the incompatibility of the two aspects of femininity as analysed by Jones and Freud"[3] (in Birksted-Breen, 1993, p. 148). Breen argues for an understanding of femininity that encompasses both an unconscious representation of lack, that is an empty space and an unconscious representation of its "concentric" aspects, the contradiction itself structuring the feminine unconscious.

We can link these ideas directly with the structure of the clitoris as it has been more recently understood. In human reproduction, there is the baby in the uterus inside the mother, the male contribution to which arrived there via the vagina, but propelled in orgasm by the clitoris surrounding it. In accommodating a baby physically, the female mind becomes stirred up into the same concentrically circular developmental levels, new mother, within self, within infantile self, within own mother, even within grandmother. (A patient's dream in Chapter Six illustrates this perfectly.) When there is not a baby, and sexual pleasure is the aim, in the female this can be facilitated by the knowledge that there is a greater complementarity in the coming together of male and female. I began this book with an aim to find a greater balance between the sexes. This complementing of each other—sexually, functionally, and especially in parenting, emotionally—provides the means to this aim.

A brief vignette from another patient here illustrates these concepts in one small aspect.

Clinical material 2

The patient, Mrs L,[4] is an artist and a mother with a history of hypomanic breakdowns. Her son, an only child, is about five years old. They are playing with a set of Russian dolls. The boy sets them out in a line from largest to smallest. This is very linear and rational, and could be seen as the stereotypical practical male approach to the situation (Figure 5 (1)). The patient however, who comes from a large family, sets them out much more subjectively. She sees that as each new baby arrives, the previous one is at a little more distance from the mother than before (Figure 5 (2)). Having been the oldest child herself, she remembers this painfully. But to complicate her way of setting out the dolls, when her own son arrived, the next generation, her own mother died within the first few weeks. Not only had another baby come between them, now in the opposite direction (Figure 5 (3)), but the mother has fallen out of the configuration. Still these representations are linear. In reality, a mother gathers her children around her in a much more concentric fashion, illustrating the theory I have described, with the different generations represented, both internally and externally. The presence of the father consolidates this.

Perhaps it is related to the psychopathology of this woman that in her setting out the dolls, she keeps to the linear albeit more motherly constellation and doesn't gather the children around. She presented following a puerperal psychotic breakdown and then another hypomanic episode since the birth of her son. Unfortunately, her illness precluded further pregnancies, so that we do not know whether she might have grouped the dolls around the mother more intimately if she had

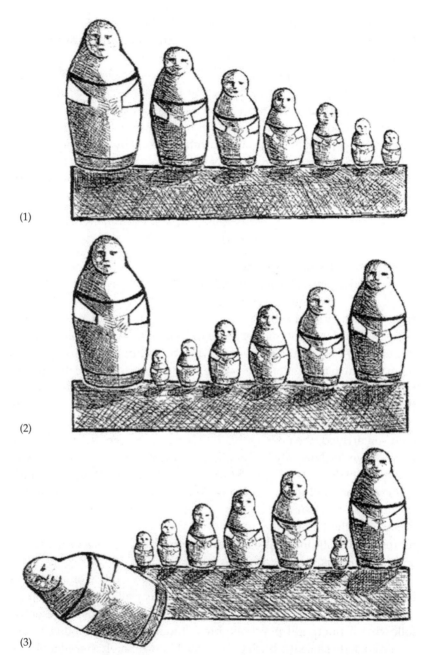

(1)

(2)

(3)

Figure 5. Russian dolls. Drawn by my patient Mrs L.

had more children. She also dropped out of treatment in a "flight into health" at a point at which her mood was again becoming unstable. Longer treatment may have enabled her to increase the depth in her relationships, but it is the nature of hypomania that sometimes a distance from the analyst has to be maintained as well.

I thought about Mrs L when I heard about Galit Atlas, who in *The Enigma of Desire* (2016) presents another distinction between masculine and feminine relating when she defines pragmatic as opposed to enigmatic aspects. She sees men as more pragmatic and women as more enigmatic and links this to their sexual organs. Those of men are mostly external, penis and testicles, though there is also the prostate, and those of women are mostly internal, uterus and vagina, though there are also the breasts and the clitoris, or a glimpse of a part of the clitoris.

A lack or a space?

Having looked at the relation to the body, I will look now at the other unconscious representation of femininity, of a lack that can also mean an empty space. To say that the female lacks a penis is skewed since she has the biological equivalent in her clitoris. The difference is that it is adapted to provide a central space. Here, the concept of the phallus, particularly as developed by Lacan, begins to sit much more clearly as relevant to both sexes, not just women. It is "a reference to the inherent lack and incompleteness of the human condition and the impossibility of total fulfilment" (Birksted-Breen, 1996, p. 650). The phallus is the object of desire that no-one has. It refers to a state of completeness and absence of need which can never be attained; or "that which the infant imagines its mother wanting" (Kohon, 1999, p. 10).

Birksted-Breen has introduced the concept of "penis-as-link" as differing both from the penis in reality and from the symbolic phallus. She says that this has a "structuring" function, enhancing mental space and thinking. The lack of internalisation of the penis-as-link leads to a compulsive search for the phallus. She emphasises how these different symbolic concepts belong to different psychic organisations. The re-instated biological information is important here because it shows that just as the female contributes her own complementary musculature, to make a shared creative platform with the male, equally, she contributes psychically to the penis-as-link. The name of this useful concept remains so male because it looks like it sounds. But another way of thinking about it now could be as the penis–clitoris link.

Conclusion

In this chapter, I have tried to utilise in my clinical work a simple shift in our biological conceptualisation of the structure of the clitoris. Also, I have tried to look at how this not only influences psychoanalytic theory now but how psychoanalytic theory, particularly in the French writing, has been close to realising the whole physical structure, previously lost down through the Ages, prior to the recent anatomical research. This is despite the traditional belief in a small clitoris and Freud's classical implication of this in his theory of penis envy. The shift is in the labelling of parts taken from the anatomical research and demonstrating how the clitoris is a much larger organ than previously thought, extending up inside the woman's body. Anatomically, it matches the penis whilst adapted to accommodate childbirth. Functionally, it responds sexually with important differences (see Chapter Two).

It is important to see how over the last century the theoretical attempts to understand female sexuality have taken on a circular pattern somehow, taking on the concentric quality and nature of the subject itself. Birksted-Breen's work (1993) is an essential contribution because it juxtaposes the biological and the psychological, making use of the innate tension. It is an example of theory trying to stay above the constant pull in the subjective response of the reader, who is poised precariously between all the frames of reference and contexts already in the literature.

The main purpose of this chapter is to show how the concentric make-up of the female is receptive to the more linear constellation of the male and that there is then a greater complementarity between the sexes. Anatomically speaking, this is apparent in the joint contributions of penis and clitoris to the sexual act, where the clitoris creates the orgasmic platform to provide support for the penis to ejaculate into the vagina. Psychoanalytically speaking, when the body (more accurately defined) is represented in the mind, the penis-as-link (Birksted-Breen, 1996) becomes much more of a structure shared between the sexes rather than one that sounds so male.

I have used clinical material, first to illustrate a common presentation that a young woman, given certain inadequacies or assaults during her development, can remain confused about the structure of her hidden excretory and sexual anatomy, resulting in the belief that she herself and sex are dirty and frightening. Also, to show that male and female conceptualisations of how mothers relate to their children can differ in relation to their anatomical make-up and its psychic representation. Atlas describes the masculine pragmatic and feminine enigmatic ways of relating that can occur in either sex, in different degrees, by linking them to the external and internal organs of *both*. But disorders such as the hypomania in Mrs L, the mother described, can neutralise the difference to a certain extent, the effect of the illness maintaining distance within the mother–child relationship and making her react in a more masculine way. Her husband hopefully could call upon his more feminine and enigmatic side to step in and parent their child.

CHAPTER FIVE

Bisexuality: a universal phenomenon*

In this chapter, it will be most evident, I think, that the bodily state and its representation in the mind can be very difficult to separate out unless one chooses, as psychoanalytic writers tend to do, only to consider the latter. The complexities of ordinary biological sexual difference, male and female, the main focus of this book, will be left to one side.

Freud defined the concept of psychic bisexuality and considered it to be universal. Men will have feminine aspects and women will have masculine aspects to their psychological make-up. But "universal" can apply in other ways. I will write from the standpoint that everyone is on a spectrum of "how homosexual", an idea that originated in a Portman Clinic discussion at the time of the AIDS crisis and prior to the subsequent cultural changes; a spectrum from "not at all" to "totally", where neither extreme will exist. At some point along that spectrum, what is purely psychic will begin to include some actual expression of the behaviours of the opposite sex, whether that is just in choice of dress,

*A shortened version of this paper was presented at a BAP conference in London in 1995, "A century of sex: developments in analytic thinking as attitudes in society change". The two conference papers were published in 1996 as a BAP Monograph, No. 8.

for instance, or sexual contact with a same-sex partner. Working with patients who are further along this spectrum of sexual or gender identity and object choice can be very informative. I will describe clinical examples first where there is biological confusion and then where there is gender confusion.

To return to Angier, one of my scientific sources, she provides a useful summary of the embryology and sets it in an anthropological frame. Each foetus starts out destined to become female unless, if there is a Y chromosome and not a second X from the father, a surge of androgen after nine weeks causes the male genitalia to develop from the undifferentiated genital ridge. Each unsexed foetus before this time has been equipped with both female Mullerian ducts and male Wolffian ducts, and whichever are not required are resorbed as the others develop. This is a relatively recent scientific discovery, but the ancients—Hippocrates, Galen, and other Greek physicians—were on to something: "They thought that the human body was basically unisexual and that the two sexes were inside-out versions of each other. The ancients emphasised the homology between female and male organs" (Angier, 1999, p. 45)—"homologue", that word from the Swedish Van Turnhout paper in 1995 (Chapter Two), obviously taken from *Gray's Anatomy*.

As each development takes place, there is opportunity for mistakes to occur, and a small number of babies are born hermaphrodite, with the organs of both sexes, or with a set of genitals that are neither one nor the other and look ambiguous. The Middlesex Hospital, now incorporated into University College Hospital along with the Royal Free, used to have a world-renowned unit where these abnormalities were painstakingly explored. Then, a multi-disciplinary team pursued the best compromise solution that the parents could bear but protecting as far as possible the child's fundamental sexual identity. This proves to be the strongest of instincts, especially if it is under the pressure of a conspiracy. These are very real problems for some parents and their doctors.

A powerful example is the adreno-genital insensitivity syndrome (AIS) in which the male end organs are insensitive to androgens. These are some of the saddest case histories I have come across. Later, I will give my own clinical vignettes in contrast to Angier's. Her case, whom she called "Jane of Arc", from New York City, had a "hernia" operation (an example of a conspiracy), when she was too young to remember. She had a scar, and then as a teenager she had endocrine follow-up. This was because she would need to take hormones long term, to protect her bones, to keep her generally healthy. Oestrogen was given because she had been designated a girl. At this point, she was told that she had had "twisted ovaries" removed at birth so she would be infertile (the conspiracy deepens). But the medics were always extremely interested to examine her, a surprise to Jane when, as she thought, the visual problem was long gone. She dwelled on her problem intellectually and tried to read up on it in libraries at university: "she read descriptions, and she knew the truth immediately and absolutely. She had what was then called testicular feminisation [now called] AIS" (Angier, 1999, p. 29). At birth, her external genitalia were female but her internal labia were missing, her vagina was short and blind-ended, there were no uterus or fallopian tubes and no ovaries. The "twisted ovaries" were undeveloped testes that had herniated downwards into her pelvis, and these were removed ten days after birth. The testes had worked *in utero*, secreting the hormone testosterone and secreting Mullerian (female) inhibiting factor. But the receptors had not responded to the hormone so that the Wolffian (male) system had not developed, and her condition had reverted to the female "default". Jane, who was XY, had inherited on her X chromosome a mutated, non-working version of the androgen receptor gene. The problem in life for Jane was her infertility, leaving her feeling empty and engulfed in her loneliness. She discovered a support group in the UK of other patients and joined it. It helped enormously.

I like to think that back then, at the end of the last century, it might have been some of my own patients whom she linked up with.

In my long years at the Portman Clinic, I treated two women with AIS. One was very like Jane. Miss J was intellectually accomplished in a high-flying job, but infertile and lonely. She was, however, there at the very beginning of dating online! She fought for surgery to fashion a full-length vagina, at least to function sexually. I admired her. But because of the particular conspiracy of her own childhood that she felt so keenly, this was repeated in that the men she met would not know she was not "normal". Until maybe she met Mr Right …?

Angier spells out the whole complicated theory of hormone receptors. I will here state my understanding, which is that the androgen secreted by the testes *in utero* (formed because of a gene on the Y chromosome), works on the receptors of all the tissues of the body resulting in male characteristics, with the help of an androgen receptor protein (formed because of a gene on the X chromosome), that enables the tissues to sense the hormone. In AIS, the gene on the X chromosome is faulty. I wonder if this can also be a partial situation, that some tissues have receptors dotted with the protein, and some, the actual genitals, do not. We are dealing here with what is often called "mosaic" pathology (Angier calls her chapter "The mosaic imagination"). My second case, Jo, seemed to illustrate a partial loss of receptors because she was so masculine.

Jo was not operated on at birth; she was not diagnosed until she was eighteen. She had grown up to be a virile sort of girl who had enormous strength, and she had reached national standard as a sportswoman. Literally, she had masculine strength. She was fit, happy, and accomplished in her sport. But her mother was worried because her periods had not started by her mid-teens. She was investigated, diagnosed to have AIS, and then had her "hernia" operation. The conspiracy was maximal because the doctor told her mother the situation but they decided to keep it from Jo, who after all was carefree.

What happened after her operation was that she lost her strength. Her sporting prowess failed and she became profoundly depressed. It was by all accounts a psychotic depression from which she recovered, and she later came for psychotherapy to deal with her loss and her anger. She too had the strong urge when recovering to frequent libraries to try to understand what had gone wrong. She too came across testicular feminisation and AIS and confronted her mother.

She worked hard in treatment to come to terms with her situation and decided what she would like. She persuaded the endocrine doctors to stop giving her oestrogen and to prescribe testosterone in an attempt to get back her sporting ability, and in any case she liked being like a man. She told me that the doctors had said that the difficulty was that less was known about the long-term effects of prescribed testosterone (in those days), and it was feared it would be carcinogenic.[1] Jo was willing to take the risk in her own time.

Laqueur, in *Making Sex: Body and Gender from the Greeks to Freud* (1990), describes the ideas of Galen as "phallocentric", taking the male pattern as primary and describing the female from that reference point (in Angier, 1999, p. 45). Each foetus has either male or female potential. But if the testes do not secrete Mullerian inhibiting factor, then a female foetus will develop. Freud's cornerstone, as Raphael-Leff puts it, was "that in the Unconscious, un-shackled from our bodies, we are psychically bisexual, and like Milton's spirits, within our minds can 'either Sex assume, or both'" (Raphael-Leff & Perelberg, 1997, p. 237). This frees up a space for psychoanalysis but also addresses the earliest of beginnings as outlined in embryology and the chances of ambiguous development as well as the embodiment of the mind that is nevertheless a part of the whole. Jane, Miss J, and Jo "knew" they were supposed to have been men. Jane and Miss J adapted to being like women, while Jo preferred to be like a man in terms of her strength, even if she had to be like a woman anatomically.

Approaching the millennium, in 1995 there was a conference in London, "A Century of Sex", organised by the British Association of Psychotherapists (BAP).[2]

I was asked, along with a GP/Jungian psychotherapist, Elphis Christopher, to speak at the conference, celebrating Freud's original work and its consequences in the development of understanding and theory. I chose as my title "Bisexuality: a universal phenomenon". My contribution was, in retrospect, from a rather narrow angle and from the extreme. In the same way that the AIS patients, at the extreme in their physical sexual presentation, are useful to learn from, the feminisation in some homosexual men who also presented to the Portman Clinic captured my interest and imagination. There were more of these patients at that time than now because it was before the shift in culture and the law that occurred at the millennium. From these extremes, it is often possible to understand better the more usual presentations. Elphis, meanwhile, presented an historical overview that was much broader-based but, continuing the "universal" theme, she then gave a case history of a couple where bisexuality was also a focus. She began with a reminder that the twentieth century had begun with an epidemic of venereal disease, notably syphilis, and that it had ended with the AIDS crisis; that before changes in the law, backstreet abortions had been rife; that the Pill had allowed women to take more control over their sexuality. Even so, having begun with mass killings in the two world wars, the century ended with a population explosion. The external factors in relation to sexuality remain the reality. She recounted her experience as a psychosexual family planning doctor where she believed that the vaginal examination created an opportunity to understand the woman's unconscious views about her sexuality. She ended by giving a case history of a successful couple that had lost interest in sex, he becoming impotent. She saw the woman as too connected to her animus, the masculine, and the man as more identified with his feminine anima. They both over-valued the masculine and attacked the feminine. The task was to restore Conunctio, Jung's term for the union of opposites. This took place inside Elphis, the therapist, who processed the characteristics of the four parents, managing an internal intercourse between a father and a mother, having survived being destroyed or seduced by either of the couple. Earlier, she had spoken of Freud's "fathering" of psychoanalysis and Klein's and other female analysts' "mothering" of it.

My own contribution began with a complicated discussion of how complicated the subject of sex is. I turned to Laplanche and Pontalis:

> Masculinity/Femininity: the way the subject situates himself vis-à-vis his biological sex is the variable outcome of a process of conflict ... the decisive factor in the assessment of behaviour from the point of view of the masculinity–femininity dichotomy is in the underlying phantasies which psychoanalysis is alone able to uncover.
>
> (Laplanche & Pontalis, 1983, p. 243)

Their definition of sexuality is then quite broad, embracing this and all the components of sexual activity that go beyond genital functioning or fulfilling basic biological needs, as well as, of course, object choice. They do not define gender separately.

Gender is a biological and not a psychoanalytic term, derived from "genus", a collective heading under which there are common overall attributes such as male and female, which then further classifies different species and more specifically families. In some languages, nouns are designated masculine, feminine, or neuter, which could be seen as a parallel with bisexuality. Gender identity will be determined by a variety of multicultural phenomena, and in *The Gender Conundrum*, Greenson's chapter refers to the establishment of gender as relatively nebulous, listing three basic determinants. These are: a) awareness of anatomical and physiological structures (Greenacre adds, primarily the face and the genitals); b) assignment to a specific gender by the parents and other important social figures; and c) a biological force present from birth which can (described by Stoller in transsexuals and illustrated by the AIS patients above) be strong enough to counteract both a) and b). Greenson adds a fourth, d) the disidentification from mother and the identification with father in boys which, of course, mother must allow (Birksted-Breen, 1993, p. 262). Stoller's idea is that it can be the unconscious wish on the mother's part for her son to be a girl that contributes to the childhood creation of a transsexual and an explanation for their names so often being sexually ambiguous (for example, Toni, Nikki).

The Gender Conundrum starts with Freud's statement, "It is important to understand clearly that the concepts of 'masculine' and 'feminine' whose meaning seems so unambiguous to ordinary people, are amongst the most confused that occur in science" (1993, p. 1). Birksted-Breen says, "As with femininity, Freud felt that, although fundamental, the concept of bisexuality was impregnated with obscurity" (p. 231). Leaving bisexuality, about which she says that there is relatively little written, until the last section, she begins there with "Bisexuality brings to the foreground again the question of the relationship of body and mind, of biological bisexuality and psychological bisexuality" (p. 231).

Birksted-Breen puts forward that there is a duality in Freud's work; this does not mean that he was confused or changed his mind, but that the duality has a purpose of its own to contain the tensions that have existed in the debate about sexuality throughout the twentieth century. She suggests that the concept of bisexuality reflects the duality "used at times to express the biological predisposition of the human individual, while at other times Freud used it to refer to the balance of object relationships" (p. 231).

Birksted-Breen argues for an "out-of-focusness" to be tolerated in our understanding of masculinity and femininity. The "out-of-focusness most clearly ... expresses the duality of Freud's position; body and mind are connected, but not completely, and the disjunction between them is difficult to grasp" (p. 5). Acknowledging that "human nature is inherently bisexual", she says that "bisexuality ... (a biological concept) is equally imbued with this bifocal vision ... (but is also considered by Freud) ... in terms of identification and Oedipal positions" (p. 5). Lacan takes this to the extreme, upholding "that masculinity and femininity are independent of biological reality, that they are constructed from the moment of recognition of sexual difference" (p. 11). Birksted-Breen sees bisexuality, then, not as an explanatory solution but as a working tool, useful in conjunction and in tension with the concept of the Oedipus complex.

These ideas perhaps characterised the general flavour of inquiry as the last millennium was approached. I came across a similarly modern approach to a related phenomenon that had occurred some decades earlier but was reported in the press around the time of publication of *The Gender Conundrum*. It serves to introduce my case examples, which by their nature will lend an air of prurience and with it a need for respect, discretion, and confidentiality.

The article was headed: "Even the wife of the president of the United States sometimes had to stand naked." It was written by Ron Rosenbaum (*The Independent*, 21 January 1995). He told the story of W. H. Sheldon, anthropologist and director of the Institute for Physique Studies at the University of Columbia until 1969, who produced an "Atlas of men". A planned "Atlas of women" was described as "ill-fated". Men and women students had been photographed naked and catalogued, but there had been an eventual realisation that this could lead to "insur-mountable psychological problems" and a re-shoot of the women was not allowed in recognition of this. More recently, only the negatives were released for scrutiny, and Rosenbaum tried to restrict his gaze so that he only glanced at the faces. He saw a crucial difference between the men and the women. The men were diffident, oblivious, but the women looked deeply unhappy, pained at being subjected to the pro-cedure, with grimaces and looks of pronounced discomfort and anger. Rosenbaum's understanding of the fact that only the negatives were available was that:

> a fascinating distinction was being exhibited here, a kind of light-polarity theory of prurience and privacy that absolves the negative image of the naked body of whatsoever the transgressive power it might have in a positive print. There is an intuitive logic to the theory, although here the Sheldon posture-photo phenomenon exposes how fragile are the distinctions we make between the sanc-tioned and the forbidden images of the body.

I think that there is a lot in this and that the use of seeing and the physics of light in understanding sexuality and sexual difference in both Birksted-Breen's and Sheldon's ideas is very interesting. My favourite theory of perversion is in fact Hans Sachs' idea that the highly specific details of each individual perversion are refracted through a prism of light called the Oedipus complex at puberty so that their roots in childhood experience cannot be traced. This is except by painstaking and lengthy work in psychoanalysis or psychoanalytic psychotherapy, of the kind so beautifully written about by Joyce McDougall (1972). We owe Sachs' translation from the German to William Gillespie (1956).

But I do not think that it is as simple as women being different from men, as Rosenbaum suggests. The subjects at Columbia were, on the surface, ordinary healthy young students. The patients I will present here are all men but with various kinds of female identification in phantasy which becomes explicit in the psychoanalytic setting and in behaviour, where it often takes the form of an exhibitionistic hostility towards women. To go back to Birksted-Breen:

> it is, from a psychoanalytic perspective, the underlying Phantasy which determines whether an act is masculine or feminine. But the phantasy takes the body as its foundation and incorporates bodily characteristics and sensations. Understanding masculinity and femininity means understanding that interplay which means tolerating the out-of-focusness.
>
> (Birksted-Breen, 1993, p. 38)

Limentani's "To the limits of hetero-sexuality: the vagina-man" (also collected in *The Gender Conundrum*) describes men who are overtly heterosexual but who have areas of darkness within that. (He is playing on Freud's "dark continent" of female sexuality here.) He notes a striking oral quality in their promiscuity and uncovers a secret wish to be a woman with a profound envy of everything female. He names the vagina-man as the counterpart to the phallic woman and recognises the latter in his object choice. Limentani feels that "the greater freedom engaged in by both men and women in expressing their desire to cross boundaries of sexual genders has encouraged the bringing into consciousness of fantasies until now subjected to denial, suppression and repression" (in Birksted-Breen, 1993, p. 274).

He makes an important plea to psychoanalysts, whom he felt were not yet absorbing the lessons from the studies on transsexualism, that is still relevant today more the fifteen years on, though the internet may have helped: "Is it not to be expected that many men could prefer to indulge in perverse fantasies of belonging to the other sex, avoiding fear of castration, and worst of all, mutilation of their bodies?" (Birksted-Breen, 1993, p. 274).

Patients with gender confusion are seen at the Portman Clinic. How do they negotiate the toilets at the entrance, passed before reception is reached and labelled "Male" and "Female"?[3] This is all part of a baseline reality and socially based culture of our times, incorporated into the psychoanalytic setting. (But it is a practice that is diminishing in favour of the rights of the disabled so that, where space is at a premium, there is often now one large unisex facility in public places.) In the old days, one patient did not make it even as far as the reception. Instead, he went home and then attended his second appointment. But the transvestite patient described below arrived cross-dressed, a relatively rare occurrence at the Portman and encouraging in that most patients are already able to put the problem into words rather than behaviour, although it would not be known if he was wearing female underwear so never shake hands … since the handshake is a business-like expression of trust as well as a greeting, we clinicians never shook hands with patients at the Portman, since their pathology was bound to include an element of deception somewhere. This upset many patients greatly and often formed the basis of the second consultation. In not appeasing their anxiety with a handshake, it in fact facilitated the often difficult psychoanalytic process, but it could be extremely painful for such narcissistic personalities. This patient delighted in using the door marked "Female" and so upset the female receptionist. Whereas the first patient was overcome by his anxiety, the second was reducing his anxiety and expressing his unconscious hostility towards women. The narcissism is easily visible, there is no regard for the Other here at all; the unconscious expression of the attack is witnessed in the discomfiture of the receptionist.

Case histories

The patient, Mr H, was wearing tight jeans and a leather jacket but had long, bright-red, feminine hair, long painted fingernails, and eye make-up. As we've noted, he went into the toilet marked "Female" which upset the receptionist. The male referrer had written a one-line letter enclosing someone else's previous summary. This is not a patient with whom many people would find it easy to engage.

He stayed for only twenty minutes into our interview, side-stepping my attempt to interpret his social transgression (really the attack on the feelings of the receptionist), and he left in disgust, with the idea of attending a gender identity clinic that offered gender reassignment instead. The tension on both sides at this initial visit left me with the expectation that I would not be seeing him again, but a year later he returned. This time, he brought with him an assessment report from the other clinic that said he did not want a sex change operation and that he was still interested in a psychotherapeutic approach to his confusion. On this occasion, his hair was black and his general appearance was more unisex than before. He stressed that he was now an art student and that the college could tolerate, in fact encouraged, his flamboyant appearance. (This reminded me of a friend of mine, a teacher in an art college, who, struggling with a similar student, felt together with her colleagues that the only thing they could do when he graduated would be to appoint him to the staff!) Mr H was less anxious than at our previous meeting and willing to explore his background. At the first interview, he had repeatedly taken long swigs of water from a large bottle, but on this occasion, though he held a small bottle in one hand and a banana in the other throughout, he kept them for afterwards.

By now, he was twenty-three years old. He had been brought up in a family where the father was strict and induced fear and trepidation in the children, a father too frightening to identify with. A scenario emerged, of the family at the meal table in silence, the patient eating nothing but instead immobilised by fear. He was acutely aware, waiting in anticipation for the "screech" of a knife and fork across someone's plate. As he remembered it, he flinched visibly, over and above his general twitchiness. As well as indicating more control over his oral needs, this time he was indicating a fear that took away his appetite.

I observed him with his oral needs catered for, this and his whole manner exhibiting how desperate his needs were, yet how ambivalent he was about dependence. I felt that the impression on me that his appearance made recreated the family meal time situation, though he was making himself into a terrified personification of the screech of a knife across a plate. Dressed as a woman, carrying a banana, he displayed visually the extent of his gender confusion and that his problem was pre-oedipal. At the same time, by projective identification, he could induce in the countertransference the feeling he would have had as a frightened little boy at the table. His appearance and his broken, complaining manner of speaking expressed this sexualised aggression in what I found myself thinking of as a screeching hysteric.

In this state of desperate need, defended against by only being able to stay twenty minutes and then come back a year later, is an example of Glasser's "core complex": a deep conflict involving a wish for union which, if it's possibility comes into view, stimulates a fear of annihilation and a need to withdraw. Developing a perversion then attempts to achieve independence in the face of the threat from the annihilating mother. (Where was she when father was so frightening?)

This patient lived at the time with a young woman who appeared to tolerate (or deny) his need at times to go off with young men. He was perplexed about the meaning of his homosexual experience; it had the quality of experimenting. He was quite clear that his girlfriend was important to him. We discussed treatment options. He was most interested in a group for transsexuals. But since most of the other patients in the group were post-operative transsexuals, it seemed more appropriate to offer him a place in a group for mixed perversions that I ran, if the other patients could tolerate him. What happened next I found very moving. He missed the first group and then in response to a letter, came to see me again immediately prior to the next week's group. We worked on his anxiety and he managed to arrive at the group, relatively calm, reflective, and engaged. He was well received. A colleague who was "standing by" in view of the other new patient at the time with a history of violence, happened to see Mr H going in. Later, he commented on his "yellow hair". I was surprised. Relative to his appearance at our first meetings, this patient now looked to me almost "normal", his anxiety and his need to act out having subsided enough to allow him to accept help.

At the conference, I decided to explore the concept of "camp" before describing two homosexual patients. Interesting and elusive, bound up in the history of homosexuality when it was illegal so that there had been a "code", I relied on Susan Sontag's essay "Notes on Camp" (1964) in which she commented on its elusivity, describing it as "a sensibility ... a variant of sophistication but hardly identical with it" (Sontag, 1964, p. 515). The history is beyond the scope of this book now, but I arrived at the idea of "a foot in both camps" as an indication of the ambivalence. She continues with a warning: "To talk about Camp is therefore to betray it ... (or at best), one runs the risk of producing a very inferior piece of Camp .... If the betrayal can be defended it will be for the edification it provides, or the dignity of the conflict it resolves" (p. 515). I present my case histories in this spirit.

At the time, the Portman Clinic was interested in Nancy Chodorow's questioning of heterosexuality as the "norm", in "Heterosexuality as a compromise formation: reflections on the psychoanalytic theory of sexual development" (1992). This was a very freeing position from which to begin a discussion. We arrived at an understanding that everyone has to have a certain amount of homosexuality in order to function and that heterosexuality is then an achievement following a struggle, more of a struggle than to stay with the homosexuality. As with many things, there can then be thought to be a continuum, of how homosexual does each one of us remain? This was a useful discussion and not in any way a definition of the causes of homosexuality. Given the origins of biological sexuality described earlier in this chapter, this is far more complicated.

In the psychoanalytic setting, these issues give rise to the problem of the interaction of the negative transference, buried in the double meaning of the camp and the illusion of the distorted reality, with the negative countertransference, which if not addressed will be directly detrimental to the therapeutic process.

Mr G

Mr G is in analysis. He professes to be homosexual, though he is nearing his mid-thirties and has as yet had no sexual experience. He is not particularly camp but he sweeps about dramatically. He is extremely narcissistic. It was autumn and he was becoming afraid of the dark. For some reason, I resisted turning on the light. He says, "You are not exactly going to be enraptured by the sight of me in the moonlight. Very 'Act One, *La Boheme*'. Except that makes you Adolpho and me Mimi. He throws back the curtains and sees her outside in the moonlight and he is enraptured. Very romantic." Mr G is both enhancing and at the same time denigrating the romance. Mr G at other times is Brunhilde in *Die Valkurie*. Once he sang to me from Act Two quietly and movingly (though perhaps I am fooling myself that he is singing to anyone but himself), associating afterwards to his mother singing nursery rhymes and old music hall songs to him when he was little. How he yearns for this still, and how his identification with his mother as his only way of staying close to her comes out in his singing that more usually is something he does to himself during his lonely weekends.

Mr G was brought up in a loving family—his parents, himself, and a younger brother. Most people have the experience of the arrival of a sibling and each weathers it according to their own personality and resilience. Mr G never really came to terms with why his parents should want or need another son when he was four years old. The brother grew up and married and started his own family. Mr G stayed in his own isolated world of books and music, identified with the Diva, holding down a good job but unable to form a relationship. He was melancholic, often depressed, and sometimes threatened suicide. A moment of hope came when he decided to take in a stray cat. The liaison lasted only a few days since he was unable to bear his envy of how fortunate the cat was in being fed and loved by him, a deeply maternal dilemma. He stayed in analysis for more than ten years and then considered another ten or a leaving date. He left, and I wondered what would become of him.

Melanie Klein gives a view about roots of homosexuality in *Envy and Gratitude* that reminds me of Mr G and his cat, and how that must link back to an oral problem in infancy.

> In men, the envy of the mother's breast is also a very important factor. If it is strong and oral gratification thereby impaired, hatred and anxieties are transferred to the vagina … The consequence of a disturbed relation first to the breast and then to the vagina are manifold, such as impairment of genital potency, compulsive need for genital gratification, promiscuity and homosexuality. It appears that one source of guilt about homosexuality is the feeling of having turned away with hate from the mother and betrayed her by making an ally of the father's penis and of the father.
>
> (Klein, 1975, p. 201)

Mr P[4]

Also depressed, as homosexual men seeking treatment often are, Mr P came for an allotted four years of once-a-week NHS treatment. He is in his forties and engaged in a desperate sado-masochistic relationship with a man who is alcoholic and impotent. He is deeply identified with Elizabeth Taylor and watches her films over and over. He is preoccupied with the fact that she is "on her last legs", and he lists other stars who are dying. He dresses in a macho, camp style—smart black trousers, too tight, black shoes, very shiny, white socks, white shirt, and a green anorak. His hair is slicked and his face gleams from scrubbing. He is highly perfumed. Why do I think he looks like a peacock? It is probably his strut and how he clicks his heels. He too sweeps into the room, once brandishing a very long and sharply pointed umbrella so that I felt frightened. (I have often been struck how umbrellas are never considered weapons at security checks in mental health and other custodial settings where there is considerable outside walking to be done between buildings.) He smiles aggressively, a contradiction in terms but a common illustration of deep ambivalence about feelings within a relationship. He complains incessantly so that the content becomes unimportant beside the annihilating process. In the transference, there is a repetition of the arguments that go on with his partner.

But Mr P is "innocent". Coyly, he abhors the gay scene and cannot face the reality that he has experience of sex with men who have simply knocked at his door. In his denial of his sexual behaviour, or at least of his urges, he reminds me of a female anorectic (though she would be unlikely to act out sexually) making herself pre-pubertal to avoid sexuality. He "diets" using large doses of amphetamines. He would have liked to have married, but his father was so possessive of his mother whilst he, the child, knew that she was secretly unfaithful, that he felt he could never commit himself to a woman because of the risk of losing her. The same happened when he fell in love with a man for the first time and found it unbearable because it made him "want the earth". (Here is an example of the insatiability of feminine desire.) This showed itself in the transference where he complained that since he did not get from me what he needed, he would have to come for ever, but then, after three years, when we discussed a leaving date in a year's time, he dropped out almost immediately.

Mr P's appearance, apart from being "camp", suggests a need to cleanse himself inside and out and this, together with his wish to remain "innocent", are evidence of the crushing superego that haunts and persecutes him. He has to maintain a deep split in his ego between what he does and knowing about it. My most difficult problem was in assessing his affects that are layer upon layer and distorted, largely by the quality of the "coyness". Whilst he has a "heightened awareness of certain complications of human feeling" (Babuscio, 1978, p. 18), this is narcissistically determined and, at another level, he appears numb and isolated, out of touch with real feeling. He is a man pretending to be a woman who is a virgin, who is shy, fearful, but titillated, but within that, pretending to be a virgin. So far, I have put "innocent" and "coy" in inverted commas. Susan Sontag says that, "Camp sees everything in quotation marks. It is not a lamp but a 'lamp'; not a woman, but a 'woman'" (Sontag, 1964, p. 519). Her choice of examples is interesting since Mr P had a "lamp" shaped like a "woman" and when his partner bought him another identical one to make a pair, he rejected it as not the same because he had not chosen it himself. "To perceive Camp as objects and persons is to understand Being as Playing a Role. It is the farthest extension, in sensibility, of the metaphor of life as a theatre" (p. 519).

The coyness relates to the false affects rather than achieve the real affects it processes, the otherwise unmanageable affects. In the countertransference, this is received as an irritatingly provocative naivety.

He is "shocked" by gay puns and soft porn movies; he is "shocked" on finding that his neighbour, whom he thinks of as an old woman, is only a year older than him; and he is "shocked" by my interpretations. Occasionally, he shows real affects. The most prominent is a white-faced rage with his eyes narrowed and his mouth foaming. When he returns after he has missed several sessions, it expresses a projection of his feeling of rejection by me. Christopher Bollas, in "The structure of evil", speaks of "malignant innocents", those who are

> unconsciously and hysterically trading on the truth ... who may insist upon absolute innocence of the self throughout life and who designate certain objects (mothers, fathers, "men", homosexuals or whatever) ... [I insert myself as Mr P's therapist] ... as perpetual villains, trade off the sympathy and need that all of us have to believe in the necessity of innocence.
>
> (Bollas, 2011, p. 167)

Mr P's family relationships are difficult, and he feels no sense of closeness or familiarity in contact with his mother, brother, and sisters. (His father died shortly before and perhaps precipitating his treatment.) When his brother unexpectedly committed suicide, he was subdued and upset but not as upset as the rest of the family, from whom he continued to maintain a distance. Instead, he dealt with his feelings by staying in his flat and watching Liz Taylor on video. "She is much more like family. An 'everyday' figure, unlike my brother." Here is an example of Mr P's use of a media figure to create a more acceptable "reality" than the painful one.

In this chapter, I have outlined my particular clinical experience with the phenomenon of bisexuality, a universal basis to male and female alike in an infinite combination of variability. This experience, for instance with the relatively extreme examples of intersex, transsexuality, and camp homosexuality, serve to underpin gender dysphoria or just gender preferences in us all. Camp is important historically, so that when homosexuality was against the law feelings and interactions could be expressed but secretly contained within a code. It offers double meanings and deep ambivalence. Nebulous and elusive, a sensibility rather than an affect, it complicates the therapeutic relationship which strives to address truth and reality, having explored the madness. It is part of the deception within the homosexual who has to outwit his superego and his objects to avoid the unbearable conflict of annihilation or engulfment, Glasser's "core complex" (1979).

Understanding the double meaning of such behaviour and its derivation will help find interpretations that are not judgemental or disapproving, and so detrimental to the neutrality of the setting by becoming superego-ish. At the same time, work with individuals such as Mr G in his analysis and Mr P in once-a-week psychotherapy can be colourful and alive, so much easier in a sense than work with the lifeless kind of heterosexual who is steeped in obsessions in an unconscious attempt to keep the lively homosexual part of himself at bay.

The sadness of the intersex patients and the deep melancholy of the transsexual ones, especially post-operatively, is reason enough to address these issues from a psychoanalytic viewpoint. The transsexual may be encapsulating his psychosis in a wish for a sex change, but to undergo surgery and believe he has joined the opposite sex forces the clinician to collude and offers only a lifetime of more generalised madness. The occasional "happy" one can only inflict the damaging consequences to mental health on the future generation, the children who have to adapt to Daddy becoming a second "Mummy".

To end on an extreme note, of interest are the patients who, when incarcerated in high security following misdeed, usually killing, choose to spend their time living as the opposite sex, pursuing a sex change. While other patients are preoccupied with their lawyers over their offence, or simply with their day-to-day chores such as how to get their washing done, the transsexual has found a way to challenge the authorities over human rights—where to be housed in the segregation thought to be appropriate today for this vulnerable population: with the men or with the women? The authorities seem willing to collude with what is really an encapsulated psychosis. There are many questions still to answer. In fact, there is currently an "epidemic" of transgender phenomena much more widely based among young people and needing desperately to be properly understood.

CHAPTER SIX

Motherhood: the fundamental aim

Of course, it is an old-fashioned idea that sex is for procreation, but this is a book about biology, so it is relevant in that sense. The evolutionary path along which the space for a baby is created by the sexual organs remaining inside and hollowing out is described in Chapter Two. The representation of this in the mind then creates the generational line of baby within mother, within grandmother, an experience much accentuated during childbirth and the puerperium. We do what our mothers did, informed by what we saw of our siblings, but also remembered from what our own bodies received and, archaically, influenced by what previous generations contributed.

This is a book dedicated to my own mother. She was a model of Winnicott's reverie, and she taught all her children about love by pure example. She dedicated her life to the long-term wellbeing of her large family. But she also longed to have had more education. She was born in a time when that was just not possible, because of the Second World War and the consequences of that for her family of origin, so that she was needed at home, and because she was a woman. She doubted her expertise as a mother, felt that she learned the hard way by experience, but perhaps a major part of her difficulty, again living in the time she did, was ignorance. Sex and the workings of one's female body were not talked about, not understood properly, even thought to be unclean in the religious sense. I remember my mother in the 1950 or 1960s being invited by the Catholic Church to a purification ceremony after childbirth and before returning to Communion. It had a celebratory aspect but it was about being cleansed. Here is the concept of the Abject again (Perelberg, 2015).

Another religious phenomenon, an extraordinary paradox, is relevant here, as it was back in the 1960s when the oral contraceptive "Pill" was born. The Catholic Church was so concerned that it researched an alternative form of birth control already in practice that it found acceptable. The "safe period", or the "rhythm method", was theoretically sound but impossible to rely upon. Either irregularity of the menstrual cycle or the sheer human nature of desire undermined its effectiveness. But how paradoxical that in a reactionary move the Church should take the stance of informing itself about the actual workings of the female body, a truly innovative step.

The focus of my book, on how the anatomy can be interpreted, I think helps to open up all the aspects of the history, whether it is the pleasure that many women find so hard to discover, or the difficulties encountered at each stage of the reproductive cycle and of having a baby. Women in earlier times were much more at risk of having no idea of their hidden make-up, leaving them with a cloacal muddle as the representation in their minds, illustrated by my patient in analysis, Miss K (in Chapter Four). For many would-be mothers, and for a variety of reasons, there may be problems. Infertility has many emotional aspects, labour can be difficult and painful, breastfeeding may not establish properly, bonding with the baby can be disturbed by puerperal depression.

I wrote my first paper long ago on the vulnerability of the new mother and the possibility of depression.[1] Not the third-day "blues" caused by the hormonal upset that in the extreme can lead to an organic psychosis, but the failure to bond and care for the baby properly that tends to become clear when the baby is about a month old. He or she still has not smiled in recognition of all that the mother is doing for them. The new mother is desperately tired. It is a time of challenge. The starting point of that paper was Winnicott's idea of moral masochism, when the mother forgoes pleasure in anything, in her baby, in the re-finding of sex, in herself, and can only pursue a strict superego approach to the attainment of cleanliness and control by punitive means. Then, the focus of my paper was on Lomas's idea that the mother envied the good that the baby was receiving from her or, where illness is serious, the good that she cannot even give because of the unbearable envy that might ensue. These problems inevitably stem from the mother's own childhood experience of being mothered, as was so clear with Mrs A and Mrs B at the Cassel Hospital, where Dr Roger Kennedy, renowned writer himself and joint editor of the book in which my paper appeared, ran the ground-breaking Families' Unit.

Whole families, usually having broken down after a new baby, were admitted to the unit. The fathers could go out to work from the hospital, older children could attend school, and those family members thought to be in need were offered psychotherapy. Most importantly, the mothers could be helped by nurses to mother their new babies. In keeping with the psychoanalytic model, everyone where possible went home for the weekends. (I also remember a family where there was only a seventeen-year-old daughter. She was the designated ill one, still the new baby so to speak. She could not separate from her parents, who were therefore both admitted with her until they could be discharged and she continued successfully on one of the young adult units.) Sadly, today resources are such that the Families' Unit is gone and there is only a much smaller contingency of young adults at the Cassel hospital.

Mrs A comes back to me as if it were yesterday:

> She is very fragile, is slow and tearful and only brightens up at the mention of her older child, a little daughter whom she tended to look to for mothering. She seems to want to be in control and a perfect mother, maybe denying feelings of not wanting to be a mother and any negative feelings she has for the children. This is especially apparent around mealtimes. She gets very anxious then and finds it difficult to control the elder child and to meet the baby's demands. She feels panicky almost at screaming point, then has to sit down quietly for a while to calm down.
>
> (Zachary, 1986, p. 189)

Mrs B is more hazy after the passage of time. It is the atmosphere within and around the couple that I remember because it was explosive. One day, we took them on a home visit.

> The relationship between the couple is very stormy and it is difficult to be with the two of them when they start to argue, particularly on a journey with them by car. The home visit became more difficult the

> nearer we got to their house and once inside the argument developed
> in full flood. Meanwhile Mrs B was continually washing her hands
> whilst ordering Mr B to remain confined to certain parts of the house.
>
> (Zachary, 1986, p. 201)

Obsessional defences and difficult, difficult ….

I will add a word or two here about the husbands since they were also admitted to the Cassel as patients. Mr A was a warm and support-ive father, trying desperately to hold down his job while supporting his depressed wife as best he could. Mr B was more a part of the joint pathology as indicated in the story of the car ride. He had an aggres-sive air about him generally. He fulfils Klein's theory about male envy of the breast and the womb as a natural progression from the Freudian to Jones' view of female sexuality, so somewhat redressing the balance from penis envy (Klein, 1975, p. 201).

There are other writers since Klein who specialise in motherhood. Jan Abram brings Winnicott into the present day scintillatingly, most notably in *The Language of Winnicott: A Dictionary of Winnicott's Use of Words* (2007). Estela Welldon broke the spell of mothering being all sweetness and light in her ground-breaking *Mother, Madonna, Whore* (1988). She outlines her theory of female perversion in which the mother uses her own body and the body of her child to attack wellbeing, a powerful expression and communication of what is often unbearable feeling. The unthinkable thought that the one closest to the baby could be the perpetrator of abuse had women fainting in the lecture hall when Estela spoke, even ten years after publication. Joan Raphael-Leff has written various books, including *Pregnancy: The Inside Story* (1993, 2003) and *Spilt Milk: Perinatal Loss and Breakdown* (2000).

The subject of my book helps to open up a greater understanding of how the female body is made and how it functions in form and in mind. The incidence of hysteria, anxiety, ignorance can all be reduced by knowledge and education.

Clinical material

A patient, Mrs S, a mother of young children, illustrates some of the theories already discussed in earlier chapters. The concentricity of the generations within the psychic representation of the new mother, derived from her physical make-up, is vividly portrayed in a dream she had. She reported it at the Monday session. She had always been afraid of water, though she can swim and has been teaching her children to swim. It is what might be lurking beneath the surface of the water that troubles her.

> The dream was set in the Mediterranean. Her children were drowning. But in the dream they were not actually her children but the children of her female cousin T. She herself had another child in the dream, who was safe. He looked like her boy cousin, the brother of T. Then there was another scene, on dry terrain. This time her own son was hers but she had lost him.

The cousin in the first part of the dream is the daughter of the patient's maternal aunt. When the patient was a baby, her aunt had sometimes acted as a "wet nurse" when her mother had to be away.

The main association to the dream was felt on first waking, a painful memory that she has lost her father. (He left when the patient was a child and more recently has died.)

We discussed the dream further and her associations were to her first and rather nonchalant mention the Friday before, right at the end of the session, of two abortions, one when she was sixteen and one when she was in her twenties. I had taken this new information and the timing of it at the very end of the week very seriously as I had ended that session. Now we thought of the drowning children as the lost potential of the abortions, and the child that seemed like her first in the dream as both the reparation for and the repetition of the loss. I was struck by the detail of the family and generational confusion in the dream and in the associations (her cousin for herself, her father for her son), trying to distance herself from the trauma. First, in the dream, there is the trauma of losing her live children, and then in the associations the sadness of the actual losses of her father and also of the earlier pregnancies. As always with this patient, who is immersed in motherhood with her own creative career selflessly on hold, the generations are very fluid in her material, again expressed in the dream by the water. Visits of both her mother and her mother-in-law during this time were very emotional. Particularly in the company of her mother-in-law, feelings about who is the son of whom and who is the actual mother are intense. For the mother-in-law, it is as if there will never be a woman good enough to replace her in her adult son's life, and my patient feels like a child, excluded from the mother/son-like relationship between her own son and his grandmother(s).

Past

In northern Peru, there is an archaeological site discovered in 1987, a series of pyramids, in one of which was found buried with his entourage the Moche leader, the Lord of Sipan (approximately AD 800 and many centuries pre-Inca). The artefacts have been moved to a place of safety in an impressive museum in Lambayeque, now a suburb of Chiclayo, north of Lima, but with ancient connections. The ceramics and the jewellery are exquisite. The lighting is subdued, spotlights trained on the exhibits in otherwise completely darkened surroundings. One of the pots depicts a woman in labour. Viewing this exhibit was enriched by the exchange that took place in front of it. The guide Carmen, young and energetic, had been switching from Spanish to English all day as if without effort. Tired by now, this time she resorted to body language. A Peruvian adolescent girl who was with her mother was clearly affected by the piece. In Spanish, she said something like, "But she ought to be lying down". The woman was sitting bolt upright, clasped from behind by another person, probably not her husband, probably another woman. The guide demonstrated how a baby could be delivered, even from a standing position, and legs planted wide she half squatted, bouncing a little. The girl was still uneasy. We all looked at the piece intently. At the woman's feet was a neat little midwife. She was encouraging the woman to push, the baby's head was crowning and clearly visible. The piece was all of five inches high. The girl seemed more settled, her mother standing silent and calm, proudly letting her daughter speak for the group. It had been a moment of communication between generations of women down the centuries of time. Unfortunately, there were strictly no photographs allowed.

Back in Lima, we discovered the Museo Larco. According to Lonely Planet, Rafael Larco Hoyle was a dedicated collector and cataloguer of all things pre- Columbian. In the early twentieth century he painstakingly explored the coastal areas of Peru, (one of the world's 'birth of civilization' areas), mapping the different civilizations that had lived there over the centuries from the preserved layers of rock that contained numerous artefacts. In his eighteenth century Viceroy's mansion, founded in 1926, is one of the best presented displays of ceramics, including more than 50,000 pots from Cupisnique, Chimu, Chancay, Nazca and Inca cultures but the highlight is the sublime Moche portrait vessels ... The same little birth scene that we had seen in Lambayeque features as if it was a mass-produced item. It belongs to a separately housed collection in the garden, of pre-Columbian erotica illustrating all manner of sexual activity with, according to Lonely Planet, comical explicitness. I would add, with honesty and straightforwardness. It simply shows the demonstration of love and affection as it is between human beings. These things make people laugh or shudder, they are intensely private experiences and are entitled to be so. But there is also the possibility that others may need help, may be helped (privately) by such openness and explicitness.

CHAPTER SEVEN

Femininity: the key to the box

The concept in the title of this chapter derives from Monique Cournut-Janin,[1] who uses the metaphor of the box and its clasp in her exposition on "The feminine and femininity" in the translated collection *Reading French Psychoanalysis* (2010).[2] She sees the clasp as the hymen, the secret and hidden gate to the vagina that breaks on first intercourse, hopefully when the girl is adult and ready to make her choice of a man. (All too often this natural pathway is sadly violated, in child abuse or rape, the latter on all levels from violence to date rape where alcohol and confusion distort consent.) But in my view, this author also holds the key in her writing to many of the questions raised in my book. She even resonates with my chosen cover from Georgia O'Keeffe, *Green and Blue Music*, when she says:

> Is the music of femininity therefore always played on two staves, with the phallic order in the key signature on one side, differently harmonized according to each person's psychic organization, and the feminine on the other?
>
> (Cournut, 2010, p. 640)

Joan Raphael-Leff is one of the editors of a British collection, *Female Experience* (1997). In her own paper where unlocking creativity is an important focus, she uses a similar idea of "The casket and the key". With the floribundant case of Gardenia, she is addressing the type of woman who thought that her "feminine", which Raphael-Leff develops into a concept of "generative identity", could only be realised by involvement with a man, it's key. For Gardenia:

> Introjected family ethos dictated that one was "nothing without a penis" ... "alternatives were being a passive little girl lacking any assertive initiative until attached to a powerful man; or becoming the idealized phallus ..." The analysis is "cyclical and multi-layered", with "primal concerns ... body parts and cloacal imagery of the female body interior"...
>
> (Raphael-Leff, 1997, pp. 239–240)

She reminds me of my own Miss K (introduced in Chapter Four), though Miss K thought the opposite, that she could manage without a man. For both, there is:

> an unconscious fear of the awesome mother's rivalrous wrath coupled with a poignant wish to return to a state of prelapsarian fusion ... She says, "... perhaps especially in female to female psychoanalytic treatment".
>
> (Raphael-Leff, 1999, p. 249)

In a successful outcome, an independent woman emerges with "her own resources and entitlement to self-generated access to her own 'casket'" (p. 256).

In *Female Experience*, Raphael-Leff's paper appears alongside Joan Riviere's paper "Womanliness as a masquerade" (1929). This was a paper of its time, yet it was one that was brought sharply back into focus when Margaret Thatcher came to power fifty years later, in 1979: how the men saw her, how the women saw her, how she seemed to see herself. It can suddenly be glimpsed rather differently in the sparkling facets of Monique Cournut-Janin's diamond-bright theoretical construction. Perelberg, in her Introduction to Part 3 of *Female Experience*, spells out that "the term 'masquerade' contains the central issues ... whether femininity is defined as a lack, a negative term, as a desire to be repressed or whether it has a positive definition of its own" (Perelberg, 1997, p. 224).

To return to Monique Cournut-Janin, the translation from the French is careful and very subtle. Having highlighted the hymen in "jewel box" terms, she says:

> that femininity is what the woman displays—attractive in her fin-
> ery, make-up, everything that makes her beautiful ... and deflects
> the gaze from the genital organs. As we know, the sight of these
> corresponds to the boy's first encounter with what triggers his
> castration anxiety ...
>
> (Cournut-Janin, 2010, p. 624)

She continues:

> Accordingly, femininity displays the entire body adorned, distanc-
> ing the male gaze from what would make him flee in anxiety. Femi-
> ninity can therefore be understood as the unconscious organization
> of a lure ... part of the great game of psychosexuality ...
>
> (p. 624)

In a footnote, she adds that "There is an obvious similarity here between the feminine organisation and the masculine one that strives to establish a fetish" (p. 624).

This leads into a gentle yet passionate description of the female Oedipus complex, the relationship between the mother and daughter and the way in which the mother teaches her daughter how to relate to father, especially after she becomes a woman (when her periods begin). The mother is struggling with the closeness of her own oedipal desire for the child (of either sex and as opposed to the real child) which gives rise to oedipal guilt, so that she "simultaneously transmits desire and prohibition" (p. 624). She calls it a "counter-cathexis", the taboo of any connection being made between her sexual organs and father's. In this way, the little girl learns not to stimulate the man's castration anxiety. In a vignette of a patient, Hilda, she demonstrates how, when father said to her, "Don't touch little one, you might hurt yourself" (Monique does not even use the word "masturbation"), Hilda always heard, "Don't touch what might hurt *me*" (p. 629). This confirms for Cournut-Janin "that for women it is men's castration anxiety and the concern to avoid

generating it in them that strongly characterizes the form of relationship they have with their own psychosexuality". Later, she calls this:

> a *hidden-shown* (there's nothing there, there's something
> there) ... that can avert the danger of generating male castration
> anxiety while suggesting enough of *the feminine* to stimulate desire
> in the other sex.
>
> (p. 634)

Cournut-Janin addresses the oedipal dilemma in such a way that it
explains why women have been oppressed and "owned" over the centuries. It also suggests why the female anatomy, hidden in nature, has been
kept hidden or repeatedly repressed at the same time. And why even the
psychoanalytic theory of female sexuality takes on a similar pattern and
dynamic itself as it was developed throughout the twentieth century.
Also, her approach might explain why certain cultures have practised
FGM in a concrete acting out of the hiddenness of the female organs by
literally cutting away the external evidence that there is. Cournut-Janin's
view cautions me in trying to bring something about all this to light,
namely the anatomy of the clitoris, and it offers a theoretical explanation for why the female anatomists have not been taken up more widely
on their research. This could also apply to why psychoanalysts seem to
have suddenly taken Freud so literally and left the details of biology
aside so entirely (Kohon, Parsons, Perelberg). It is unclear whether this
was, in a conscious way, parallel implied responses alongside my own
more direct one, to the the brash and salacious excitement stirred up in
the media. The timing would be exact. Or whether it is unconscious, yet
still uncannily, perfect timing. There is a passionate striving by these
psychoanalysts to keep a defined space for psychoanalysis, something
that is so difficult to do and to which I sincerely aspire. But despite the
theoretical correctness of their contributions, they would still fit into the
overall pattern of repression of knowledge of the female, apparent in
what happened over time in culture and in the wider psychoanalytic
literature. A conspiracy is too strong a word but maybe a *strategy ...*?
This is the word used by Cournut-Janin to describe the mother–daughter
transmission "for making the feminine tolerable" (2010, p. 631).

Interestingly, Cournut-Janin makes only one reference to the clitoris,
and that in a footnote (p. 625). She is referring to a concept of "primary
repression of the vagina" (Braunschweig & Fain, 1971) that describes the
relegation of the female sex organs (to be out of focus, unspoken about, as

in the mother–daughter strategy). The footnote says, "But not the clitoris, which tends to foster the phallic lure ('that will grow'… for example!)" (p. 625). Here is where looking at the sexual organs scientifically is an essential component. The clitoris will become tumescent when the woman is aroused but from being already grown and *in situ*.

Cournut-Janin's focus instead is the vagina and the "key to the box", the hymen. Is this then the last piece of the whole puzzle to be addressed in clear language?[3] I came across an American poet, Sharon Olds. She makes it a personal speciality of her own to write about the female genitalia, and I first heard her "Ode to the hymen" on the radio. It is written in copious, sororic adulation. She says she began writing Odes on hearing Neruda's "Ode to common things". Her volume (2016) contains an Ode to the vagina, an Ode to the clitoris itself, Odes to menstrual blood, to tampons … The hymen acknowledges the clitoris, it is as if they are like sisters …. The poems are raw, over-intimate, must give rise to embarrassment … To me, it begins to sound like the "mumsiness" of the recent American psychoanalytic literature on female identification with the mother … (see Chapter Nine).

To return here to psychoanalysis, Alcira Mariam Alizade has a chapter on "Virginities". This plural approach, together with the translation from the Spanish in general, makes it difficult to read. The sense seems to centre on a woman belonging to herself, very much Raphael-Leff's theme and vitally important sociologically. "One takes a psychic hymen for oneself, belongs to oneself" (Alizade, 1999, p. 116). She offers the idea of virginity being self-integrity.

> the virgin part of a subject is the intimate secret part, the territory of the unconscious properly speaking … that which is waiting to be conquered, the virgin forest of our thoughts and our desires, the area that will be deflowered in exploration and discovery.
>
> (p. 117)

One point that emerges from Alizade's account is that it is still possible to be a virgin even after the first defloration—deeper inside, so to speak. She focuses on the hymen and returns to D. Anziou (1985), his "skin-ego", and the central theory used in her work,

> covering and protecting, malleable and strong … A basic imaginary psychic space, enfolds the whole body and guards it from outrages and violence. It … can be torn but can also heal itself if it were.
>
> (p. 116)

Alizade listens to her young female analysands:

> who reveal … an injured skin-ego that desperately seeks … another skin with which to recreate a common skin and calm the painful anxiety arising from the injuries of the skin-ego—those "wounds of the soul" that will not heal …
>
> (p. 116)

Alizade describes four phases of the dissolution of the female Oedipus complex. The first is of passivity, the violence of maternal desire, a moment of primordial femininity. The second is of phallic enjoyment. Psychoanalytic theory is written from the premise that the girl does not have a penis. Even Alizade puts it this way: "In the third phase … of sexual difference … a time of penis envy … denial … 'Everyone has one' … the girl puts her clitoris in the category of penis-phallus …" (Alizade, 1999, p. 129).

I would say that "denial" here is too subjective, too strong a word. Given the revised anatomical interpretation of her inner anatomy, I want to use "deceived". But it is really about "unenlightenment", concerning the inner reality.

In the fourth stage, Alizade reaches "Affirmation" of femininity and whole-body erogeneity, "accepting castration and the narcissistic blow of 'not having' … and beyond the penis-phallus, reaching the plateau of 'not having', affirming oneself there, and simply 'being' a woman" (p. 131).

The power of the negative is a robust psychoanalytic theory in itself, but as Alizade says, "not having a penis tells us nothing about what a woman does have" (p. 131). A woman has all the symbolic signifiers she lists and the philosophical positions, such as the capacity to be alone, to which she aspires. But a woman also has her internal anatomy, structured like the penis but hollowed out to achieve the same aim at which Alizade arrives, the love of oneself and, from that, the desire to be a mother to the loved one.

To return to my first "key", Monique Cournut-Janin's orientation is to a dual register, "femininity" and "the feminine". "Femininity" is about the appearance, the gaze, and has a phallic reference; "the feminine" concerns the uterus and the internal erotic zones, motherhood, and involves the doll. She seems to have just the right emphasis, just the right level of intellectual discernment. This allows us to know about these things as much as we can know but to treat them with the respect they deserve and require, in order to maintain the health and wellbeing of our race. Desire, after all, is the very first step in the process of pro-creation. Monique Cournut-Janin is promoting the preserving of desire. Charmingly, she does it in a way that follows on from her husband Jean Cournut's chapter about why men fear and therefore dominate women, whom they might see as castrated, whom they might envy and fear due to anxiety evoked by women's capacity for unlimited sexual pleasure.

I mean this chapter to be central, to begin to draw together the biology, as it is now interpreted in our own era, and the many different psychoanalytic theories of what it means to be female.

CHAPTER EIGHT

Aggression and the female form

I will begin this chapter with some personal experience and leave it to what follows to give it some context. In our long experience at the Portman Clinic, it was evident that male patients with a history of uncontained violent acting out were generally composed and well behaved when seeking help in an outpatient setting. It is a surprisingly quiet and dignified place. This applied to female patients too, but the only serious incidents, though these were very rare, more often involved them. It happened in the most disturbed women and seemed to me to illustrate a general lack of being able to feel contained. Either there was a suggestion of hysterical outburst, it had regressive features, or it indicated personality disorder or psychosis.

In Angier's chapter, "Spiking the punch: in defence of female aggression", she illustrates the often characteristic *quality* of female aggression that in my experience too shows itself particularly in the disturbed— of secretiveness, long premeditation, and cruelty. She distinguishes between good and bad aggression. Rather than "good" aggression, psychoanalysts tend to refer to "benign" aggression following on from Winnicott (Jan Abram); Jan's example would be to eat food. Or another version is "ordinary" aggression (Angela Joyce), exemplified by the vigorous sucking of the infant at the breast. My own suggestion of such aggression is the force required in childbirth. Sport is another. According to Angier, "bad" aggression, on the other hand, is aimed to hurt, with its foreknowledge and with malice. Boys tend to kick, whilst girls are more inclined to find words in curses or barbed insults. Girls will storm off, or pretend not to exist. Girls will hold grudges, often against other girls (or I would understand this as against the mother). Girls' aggression can be woman-centred, harsh, and intimate, often expressed in the spreading of vicious rumours. Again, following my theme in other areas in this book, it mirrors the hiddenness of the female form that I will now address.

The biological and psychological roots of female sexuality interlink and characterise the expression of female aggression. The title of this chapter encompasses various important tenets, such as: that there is a particular quality to the expression of aggression by females that differs from male aggression; that the female physical form has a bearing on this; that the female physical form is in itself controversial anatomically; that there is more similarity (and here is the real challenge, to write about this coherently) between male and female organs than has until now been understood; that the body has a mind of its own (e.g., hormonal response) and that the mind also has a body of its own (e.g., representation); that the female role also contributes to the way aggression is expressed.

There is already a growing psychoanalytic literature on female aggression (Motz, O'Connor, Yakeley, Welldon)—interestingly, all female authors. It is worth including Motz's starting point still in general terms and not denoting women in particular. In *The Psychology of Female Violence*, she states Shengold's definition of violence as "a loss of control of aggressive impulse leading to action". Then she quotes Fonagy and Target, who build upon this: "Violence, aggression directed against the body may be closely linked to failures of mentalization, as the lack of capacity to think about mental states may force individuals to manage thoughts, beliefs and desires in the physical domain, primarily in the realm of body states and processes" (Motz, 2001, p. 2). She acknowledges Perelberg (1999), who believes that violent acts occur in order to rid the assailant of "intolerable states of mind".

I have put forward ideas relating to some of the different aspects listed at the beginning in other chapters of this book. Here, illustration of the link between sexuality and aggression and the particular quality of female aggression will be best made using clinical material from women who express aggression using their relationships to their bodies in different ways.

The quality of female aggression tends to be very different from the more direct nature of male aggression. It can be secretive, which seems to mirror the internal structure of the female anatomy. A potential characteristic and sinister form of cruelty then derives from the secrecy, often long premeditated. If this connection between the quality of female aggression and sexuality is understood better, it could facilitate more direct recognition of natural and healthy aggressive wishes and therefore more containment of the potential for cruelty.

Underpinning the different quality of female aggression is Winnicott's distinction between "the male element (that) *does* (and) the female element (in males and females) that *is*". He says "It seems that frustration belongs to satisfaction seeking. To the experience of being belongs something else, not frustration, but *maiming*" (Winnicott, 1971, p. 195; my italics). His essay is about the breast and its state of being, allowing the baby to develop a sense of self. Where the breast has been too active in doing (or going away), the self-identity is weakened and the body experienced at times of stress as alien. The separation anxiety that ensues must have a bearing on, for instance, cutting behaviour, so common in disturbed women. In another way, this is true for anorexia nervosa.

Crowley-Jack has interviewed many women in *Behind the Mask: Destruction and Creativity in Women's Aggression* (1999). She addresses the lack of available models by which to understand women's aggression, defining her purpose "to represent the forms and meanings of it from women's perspectives" (p. 4). She approaches depression through aggression, "a seldom used back door, much more forbidden" (p. 10). She describes aggression in ordinary usage as a "slippery and elusive" concept, at one time designating an act, at another an aspect of personality, or a way of interacting (p. 35). All these are apparent in my first clinical example.

Clinical material 1

Ms C came for once-a-week treatment. She was a single mother, herself the child of a prostitute. She expressed her aggression actively against society and had a conviction for writing graffiti, but she also attacked her own body and used her son to communicate aggressive feelings. She was extremely proud of him, and he seemed well cared for in some ways. But there were times when he seemed to have to fend for himself, and other times when he was actively having to look after his mother. He was about five years old at the time and she still in her early twenties.

Ms C herself had been brought up in care, constantly moving about, and in her teens she became seriously disturbed, out of control, and delinquent, ending up for a time in secure care. Subsequently, she had been prosecuted for writing "Nestle poisons babies" on the wall of a family centre, where she had a "crush" on a female worker. In the 1980s, Nestle had themselves been prosecuted for watering down their formula to be sold in the Third World. Ms C felt identified with those babies—no parents, no mother to feed her, and now difficulties in providing her son with what she had not had herself. This had become externalised and repeated in Freud's fundamental pattern, in that the worker whom she had idealised and now persecuted was not being seen to give her what she needed. This maternal longing was sexualised into the "crush".

At the time of treatment, she was engaged in an attempt to communicate with her mother. This consisted of "spoiling" plans with elaborate fantasies of smashing the idyllic family life with other children that she knew her mother now had. Her fantasy was that she would secretly befriend and seduce the son, her half-brother, and then think up more, gruesome ways to get back at her mother. In the event, when she did telephone and her mother answered, she melted and a constructive meeting took place.

Week by week, I felt battered by the force of these events as they unfolded and was left with concerns for the young half-brother as well as for her own son. But at the same time, she was putting herself at risk, driving whilst drunk, not eating properly, and self-abusing in various ways, about which she was ashamed and therefore secretive. But the self-abuse apparently caused bleeding, and as a result of it all, she said she was becoming anaemic, then "fainting at traffic lights". I would hear about how she had crashed her car on the way to a session, fallen asleep for hours, leaving her son unattended, or not fed the dog properly for weeks, and so on. In the transference, this could be taken up as the inadequacy of a once-a-week session and how I had to be tormented and treated cruelly in return for my cruelty, in an enactment of the punishment she had in store for her mother.

She would allow me no contact with her doctors, who were by now investigating the anaemia. In some ways, the therapy "bled to death" because when she was admitted to hospital, she could no longer attend. I visited her, but unwisely, because it broke the setting and she never returned to regular treatment. Instead, she brought her son with her to occasional sessions, complaining that there was no childcare available. The institution was then given the dilemma of either a lively five-year-old bouncing up and down for an hour in the car, directly on the main road outside, or of bringing him in to wait in the waiting room, alone with other patients. The only thing was for him to join the session, where he played and shone as his mother faded into the background, her depression now clearly visible behind the familiar aggression. She took to telephoning instead and, when this was not encouraged, corresponded, before eventually disappearing.[1]

Whereas male sexuality is very visible, external, inserting, female sexuality is largely hidden, internal, inserted into. In male perversion, much of the acting out, sexual and violent, involves directly confronting the body of another, or symbolically the mother's body in the form of, for instance, a burgled house. Ms C secretly befriending her half-brother, or putting her own and her son's bodies at risk, with the aggression channelled specifically through the feeding relationship, epitomised in the content of the graffiti, is more characteristic of female perversion (Welldon). This male/female difference in expression of unconscious intent is important because it mirrors anatomical and biological difference.

As Winnicott's example about mother and child shows, there are other juxtapositions of sex and aggression as well as the sexualised aggression that is perversion. These occur universally in childhood fantasies. The child, according to Freud, thinks that the little girl should have a penis like the little boy. This idea passes through various developmental stages, for example, disavowal, "There is a penis there, I saw it", and fantasy, "she hasn't a penis now but it will grow later" (McDougall, 1972, p. 379). The little boy worries that if the little girl doesn't have a penis, what has happened to it and, by implication, what might happen to his? Magical mechanisms of denial operate in both sexes in order to manage the overwhelming anxieties about not having a penis or losing a penis. The aggressive component is here in the unspoken detail of the anxiety of what has happened to it.

Clinical material 2

Mrs L was described in Chapter Four. Here is an extended version of her presentation.

Mrs L is an artist[2] and a mother. Her son, an only child, is about five years old. They are playing with a set of Russian dolls. The boy sets them out in a line from largest to smallest. This is very rational, can be seen as the practical, linear male approach to the situation (Figure 5(1)). The patient, however, who comes from a large family, sets them out much more subjectively. She sees that as each new baby arrives the previous one is at a little more distance from the mother than before (Figure 5(2)). Having been the oldest child herself, she remembers this painfully. But to complicate her way of setting out the dolls, when her own son had arrived, the next generation, her mother died within the first few weeks. Not only had another baby come between them, now in the opposite direction, but the grandmother had fallen out of the configuration altogether (Figure 5(3)). Still these representations are linear on paper. In reality, a mother gathers her children around her in a much more concentric fashion, with the different generations represented, both internally and externally. This is helped and supported psychologically by the presence of the father.

The concentric pattern of the mother's gathering her children around her, with the baby closest to her, illustrates beautifully the theory of concentricity described in Chapter Four. I thought of the pattern of the boy's arranging of the dolls as linear, but Galit Atlas in *The Enigma of Desire* (2016)[3] opens up this whole representational difference between the sexes in her distinction between male and female desire. The male is *pragmatic*, while the woman, in line with her anatomy, hidden and secret, is *enigmatic*.

The aggression in this clinical example is in the form of the life force itself, death occurring at the same point as new life, siblings jostling for mother's attention for their own survival. But also, this memory occurred in the treatment in the context of envious feelings arising at the birth of a step-granddaughter. Mrs L referred to her as a "step-grandchild" (her husband's grandchild from a previous marriage), to distance herself from her own lack of a daughter. Also, she meant to report that she was born by Caesarian but made a slip and said "hysterectomy", indicating the envy and aggression.

The next patient illustrates the transgenerational and "Russian doll" concentrical nature of being and relating that runs throughout this book. Also, she shows how the conflict between positive and negative aggression can be resolved in treatment.

Clinical material 3

Mrs D, a successful young businesswoman, is happily married and now, after taking longer than she had hoped to conceive, is expecting a baby. Her mother, who had a psychiatric history, was killed when she jumped under a train when Mrs D was a child. Having developed a resilient, though "cut-off", attitude to this, now that Mrs D is pregnant herself, she is worried that something frightening will be uncovered. She knows this is to do with the violence of her mother's death. Exploring the possibilities, it seemed likely that she is worried about having the kind of child that pushes her to the limit, that feeling of "I've had enough", and that she might hurt the child. "Only with words", she decides, but her next association was to "walloping" her husband sometimes, in an unexpectedly fiery response that made her wonder just whom she was "walloping". Perhaps there is a child's guilt that she drove her mother to commit suicide. Perhaps there is revenge for the legacy it has created.

Mrs D has internalised both her mother and her grandmother (who was very involved in her care after her mother's death and who has since died herself). She has the baby physically inside her body, but psychologically she also has both the mother and the grandmother inside her mind. The baby, like other babies, male and female, has a "Russian doll" of mothers.

The patient says, "I don't like it". Because in her mind she got rid of her mother in triumph when she died. She didn't want her (and all the problems of her illness), and it didn't affect her. It was a defence against the pain. Now she is pregnant, there is a transgenerational influence.

Michel Odent, the French natural birth pioneer of the 1970s, has recently added to his theories of natural birth that babies born by elective Caesarian section have difficulties with loving. That not experiencing the healthy "violence" of the natural childbirth process in relation to the mother is detrimental when the alternative is to be suddenly "cut" from the womb with clinical "violence". This does not apply to emergency Caesarians where there is mutual distress already and the lifesaving surgery relieves it, or to elective Caesarians where there is a valid medical reason, again a basis for the beginning of the mother–child relationship.

Mrs D adds to Odent's theory: it is not the Caesarian that is detrimental in itself, it is the relationship between the "selfish" mother who chooses it for her own reasons and the baby who is from the beginning, therefore, damaged. This solution will be a defence against the mother's own pain, again transgenerational. But unless there is a certain amount of the right type of aggression, she will have problems producing the child, as perhaps her initial failure to conceive was a defence against a fear of the wrong sort of aggression.

The next patient is described because, unusually, she talks about her clitoris. That word, so little used out loud until now, belongs in this book and in this chapter.

Clinical material 4

A professional woman, Mrs F had been in analysis for some years. Her children are grown up, and she and her husband have a comfortable existence. On the outside, there would not seem to be much of a problem, but internally Mrs F holds bitter resentment and demonstrates an insatiable emptiness. This is especially noticeable before breaks, and the material I will present precedes an unusually long break of which she had good notice.

Unusual in that she talks about her clitoris, my patient is interested in her body generally but occasional mention of the clitoris stands out. There is a quality to her stark labelling of body parts in general that can feel quite attacking. Also, if she arrives early for a session, she will sit outside my house, looking for new clues, trying to map the layout of the rooms inside in her mind. This also has an intrusive feel to it, as if she is trying to get right inside me. On arrival, she presents herself rather like a little mouse, defending against her strong desire to attack and penetrate.

The material consists of a series of three dream scenes presented on a Wednesday morning, shortly before the break mentioned.

> In the first dream scene, the patient visits a female friend. The friend wants sex and is pressing against her. She seems to have an erection. It must be a large clitoris. My patient says to her friend, "I am not a lesbian". She tries to escape but her friend locks the door.
>
> In the second scene that follows immediately in the session, she is on holiday with her husband and others. She feels her tongue

swelling up. She shows it to her husband urgently because she cannot speak. He looks and says, "Oh God", and, terribly shocked, he rushes her to hospital.

Thinking myself about sexualised aggression, I asked her how she thought these dreams were linked. She said that it was as if she had a penis in her mouth. Her association was to remember the early days in the analysis when an intense erotic transference had developed and she had become sexually attracted to me. She was pleased with this dream because of her statement "I am not a lesbian", as if that uncomfortable phase was now laid to rest.

I asked her why memories of that time should be coming up now. The holiday in the dream must relate to my coming "holiday", and we knew from past patterns that quite perverse material, indicating sexualised aggression, tended to appear at such times.

She told me the third dream scene.

They were in the kitchen of a shabby holiday let, washing up. The knives and forks wouldn't come clean, they couldn't get rid of the dirt.

She then mused about sexualised aggression, and I became aware of a familiar countertransference heaviness that always appeared when she introduced dirt or mess. I felt it being used to bog me down, lock me in, as her friend did to her in the first dream, so that I cannot abandon her.

This patient has led a full life, brought up children, enjoys a measure of sexual fulfilment, and has reached a certain level of maturity. Concentricity for her moves easily between the different levels of development, and she has a studied awareness of her body and its representation in her mind. However, when faced with abandonment, in particular, she shifts into a more phallic position, where the natural feminine space within her ceases to feel accommodating and creative and instead feels empty and needy. She can only attack that to which she would usually aspire—heterosexual union, as in the first dream scene of homosexual contact, and in the perverse misplaced anatomy of the second dream.

It is important to acknowledge what women can do to men as a result of their tendency to exert aggression in a secretive and cruel manner. Apart from whatever conscious reason there is in the heat of the moment, it can be both a behavioural expression of their biological make-up as well as a response to the assault over centuries by the male, culturally in supremacy. I am not arguing causally or trying to justify anything, but I know from my many years working at the Portman Clinic that however much it is wrong for men to hit women and that there is no justification for it, that in many, many examples of domestic violence towards women the trigger was that she said she was leaving him. Whether this was said in anger, fear, retaliation, hatred, or an explosive mixture of these and other feelings, the man who is psychologically minded enough to seek help will express his own vulnerability about the fear of being left as if it were his mother who was about to leave him. At assessment, there will always be a clue in his own probably traumatic history as to why he is so vulnerable. Of course, the reason the woman was leaving is relevant in each individual case.

A chapter on aggression and the female form would be incomplete without mention of female circumcision, or female genital mutilation (FGM). This really expresses aggression from without rather than, as the main focus has been, from within. Assad

> traced the custom to ancient Egyptian beliefs in the bisexuality of the Gods. The feminine soul of man was thought to be located in the foreskin and the masculine soul of women in the clitoris. Thus in initiation to adulthood the feminine portion of the male has to be shed as does the male portion of the female.
>
> (1980, in Kulish, 1991, p. 520)

This serves to illustrate the balance of bisexuality in both sexes. Male circumcision has been culturally and socially acceptable. Given the more integral nature of female anatomy in relation to the whole body, female circumcision, though expected still in some cultures, has most certainly not been socially acceptable. But there are questions about envy; that apparently in parts of Africa, it is the women who mutilate the girls as they themselves have been mutilated, certainly, the women make the arrangements; the fact that structurally, the male loses a lot less than does the female and suffers a lot less also. In my view, one of the consequences of the theory of penis envy is that it obscures and probably also accentuates the insidious and often unexpressed envy between women.

Angier wants to support the place of women in a man's world, to uphold that their strength can be a match and should be noted. I have wanted to open up the whole quality of the female form of aggression and relate it to the female form. If the unacceptable cruelty of expressions of aggression in the disturbed and disadvantaged can be addressed, then the life-giving positive form of aggression that helps women bring children into the world and then protect them can be fully realised. A mother who can recognise her, at times, near-murderous feelings towards her baby can nurture it and will not need to hurt it. Many women who seek psychoanalysis are so afraid of their aggression they are nearly paralysed from communicating honestly and spontaneously: "I want you to think I am a mouse because I don't want you to think I am a lion." I think Miss K in Chapter Four is a good example of this kind of woman. Mrs F in this chapter personifies it. They need to hide their feelings from themselves and then from others, and the risk for some (though I would not have thought for either of these) is that the unacknowledged feelings will then be expressed secretively and in a deadly fashion when left alone with a helpless dependent child or even a helpless, for instance, inebriated man. This will occur in extreme cases. Much more commonly, the feelings will be channelled into debilitating psychosomatic symptoms, but this is beyond the scope of this book.

Part III

CHAPTER NINE

Recent developments in the literature

M y focus has really been on the "storm" of the last century in the psychoanalytic literature on female sexuality and an opportunity that was missed or avoided at the end of it when biology offered a re-interpretation of the structure of the clitoris. There have been some developments in the general field of female sexuality in the literature since the millennium, though an impression is that it seems quieter. The familiar dynamic continues, of the subject seeming to disappear only to re-emerge later. My hypothesis is that this links to the character of the female genitalia, hidden and potentially frightening. But women analysts have been meeting in international groups and producing edited volumes. Examples are: *Studies on Femininity*, edited by Alizade (2003); *Motherhood*, edited by Cheshire (2007); and *The Female Body*, edited by Moeslein-Teising and Thomson Salo (2013). These books have emerged from the Committee on Women and Psychoanalysis (COWAP). Rosine Perelberg has been organizing a series of conferences on sexuality in the UK recently with an emphasis on female sexuality. Journal representation has been particularly quiet, except for a notable contribution in the dedication of much of an edition of the *Journal of the American Psychoanalytic Association* (2003) to women, where many of the contemporary names in the American field,

Tyson, Holtzman and Kulish, Balsam, Chodorow, and Kramer Richards feature. Rosemary Balsam's book *Women's Bodies in Psychoanalysis* (2012) has been extensively reviewed, and I counted six different ones.

Tyson provides an overview but concludes that Freud's dark continent is still only a little less dark (2003, p. 1119). Holtzman and Kulish continue their examination of the feminisation of the Oedipus complex in Part Two "Aggression reconsidered", and conclude "that girls and women frequently relinquish a sense of agency over both aggression and sexuality in dealing with triangular conflicts, to preserve a safe relationship with their mothers" (2003, p. 1127).

Balsam focuses on the vanished pregnant body from the theory of sexual development and suggests "that the plasticity of the female form in all its developmental phases may underlie the paradoxical requirement that stable mental representations be established upon an elusive set of shifting images" (2003, p. 1153).

Nancy Chodorow's contribution is "Too late: ambivalence about motherhood, choice and time". It addresses the current practice of late motherhood … or not, because it is left too late (2003, p. 1181).

Arlene Kramer Richards takes "A fresh look at perversion" (2003, p. 1199). It confirms the value of the diagnosis of perversion in women, and highlights the place of pleasure and aggression in its expression. I am not sure I would agree with her definition of pleasure. I think she might mean organic excitement. This can have very negative undertones or overtones. As Kramer Richards acknowledges, perversion involves debilitating compulsion, devaluing of love, coercion of objects, perhaps children. A paedophile presenting for treatment will report pain not pleasure. She addresses this in her conclusion (p. 1215) and calls it "unpleasure".

But just today (1 October 2016), as I am thinking "Is this book now finished?", another journalistic source has emerged in the *Evening Standard* (30 September 2016). Phoebe Luckhurst writes, in "Reclaiming the biscuit", about women who meet together, not psychoanalysts but those interested in crafts, and as the new face of feminism want to refute old stereotypes.

> This prescribed notion … that women should be meek, quiet, domesticated and motherly, that women are second-tier and their ideas second-rate and that men have some claim to their bodies and their minds, and their voices are more important.
>
> (Luckhurst, 2016, p. 22)

Whilst in this mode Luckhurst is apparently at home, baking biscuits in the shape of vaginas. (The newspaper picture shows simple, round biscuits with rounded but irregular shapes iced on to them in glitter.) I would like to think they are in the spirit of Van Turnhout's longitudinal representation of the clitoris in Chapter Two. Sadly, I think they are only meant to be entrances to vaginas, with all that is attempting to be conceptualised in this book again hidden. She explains that her preoccupation is connected with the publication of a book, *Crafting and Feminism: Twenty-Five Girl-Powered Projects to Smash the Patriarchy*. The book is by an American author and comedian, Bonnie Burton, undeniably earnest, yet, Phoebe wonders, can she support it? She argues that:

> baking is associated with old, regressive notions of femininity, while talking about the vagina is part of the new, graphic and corporeal movement in modern feminism—one that focuses, in large part, on the body and its effluents, precisely in order to undermine the old, regressive notions of femininity.

Much of the modern discourse, she says, is about "Reclaiming … the female body in a very ostentatious way, by noisily celebrating all its functions" (Luckhurst, 2016, p. 22).[1]

She then publicises a Norwegian album release that same day, by Jenny Hval, called *Blood Bitch*, that scrutinises the period taboo. "I want menstrual blood to have a huge, creative, real world power", Hval is reported as saying. The article is really about women's rights in the workplace, and Hval is campaigning for time off during periods. The fiercest argument about it is apparently not between men and women but between women and women where one group feels it is unsisterly not to support this right. Luckhurst is claiming some progress … It all reminds me of and gives a context for the Odes to the parts of the female genitalia of Sharon Olds (see Chapter Seven). But it is also reminiscent of *The Vagina Monologues*, a play written and performed by Eve Ensler much acclaimed in London around the millennium. Yet another fifteen to twenty years and there is the same characteristic, creative surge of energy, trying to express openly what is naturally suppressed for reasons I have tried to make clear in this book (particularly in Chapter Seven).

Back to the beginning, another journalistic source, this time reporting a sociological thrust but becoming just as caught up in the backward pull as when the re-interpretation of the anatomy of the clitoris was reported. Progress but also not progress. That attempt was lost to comedy masking fear and, sadly, more than fifteen years on again and it seems worse. Men will just laugh or be very angry, but really they are afraid ... Psychoanalysis understands this, but can it help? I hope to have offered a chance for new theory to develop.

Meanwhile, lifting this all into art, the Georgia O'Keeffe flower paintings, so like the female genitalia, despite the artist's lament against this, shout loudly from the Tate Modern 2016 exhibition .... Having chosen an abstract out of respect, *Green and Blue Music*, and using it to illustrate Toesca's work (*Journal of Anatomy*, 1996), I look back at my impasse, involving not only problems in conceptualisation and writing, but also aggravated by an anxious response until there was enough of a cultural shift, and wonder at its power. It now all seems more straightforward. (Especially having read Michael Rustin's Foreword!) No-one is saying male and female are the same. They are made of the same human tissues (apart from Toesca's exception of the valves in the penis to aid rigidity and therefore function), but constructed differently. The penis is singular and external, the clitoris is divided in the middle and mostly internal, a pair of structures joined concentrically. And as Atlas (2016) observes in her exposition on the pragmatic stance of the masculine and the enigmatic stance of the feminine, the prostate in the male is internal and therefore not usually included in the male genitalia. It is as forgotten as the internal parts of the clitoris ...

Dana Birksted Breen begins her book The Gender Conundrum with Freud's famous footnote:

> It is important to understand clearly that the concepts of "masculine" and "feminine", whose meaning seems so unambiguous to ordinary people, are amongst the most confused that occur in science.
> (Freud, Three essays on sexuality, 1905 footnote 1915, SE 7, p. 219)

I will end my book with a favourite saying of Lorna Wing, psychiatrist and pioneer in the classification of Autism, who died aged 85 in 2014. "Nature never draws a line without smudging it ..." (Gillberg, Obituary, British Journal of Psychiatry Bulletin, 2014, p. 53).

AFTERTHOUGHTS

Why did this happen now, in 2016, that I could set to and organise this book on a particular aspect of female sexuality, the biological re-interpretation of anatomy? It followed repeated unsuccessful attempts to publish in journals, despite helpful peer reviews. All this material, together with correspondence and lists of references, "littered" my files (to borrow Parker's comment about the unconscious, see Chapter Three) and built up over fifteen years.

I wanted to organise it into some more useful form. As one gets older, there is a sense of needing to reflect. My conviction was ongoing that the information contained in this book needed to be out there, inform-ing society, informing theory, especially psychoanalytic theory. Cultur-ally, it had not been the right time before, as I had experienced when I struggled to write about the menopause, also published after fifteen years of trying, in 2002. But as well as the time being right out there in the cultural environment, it also had to be right for me. I think my piece on the menopause that was published could not have happened until I had reached *un certain age*. For a whole book on female sexuality, I needed to have more space, family grown, retirement from the NHS achieved, time for a greater commitment to psychoanalysis, living life at a slower pace despite the paradox of time seeming to speed up.

Even though previously, I had received enthusiastic encouragement from anonymous journal reviewers, it seems important here to
record for the annals of history that despite interest, just how difficult
it was to find anyone who was not too reluctant or too busy to discuss
this project further or to take on any reading. This makes my personal
acknowledgements at the beginning of the book all the more heartfelt.
Crossing the disciplines is always difficult, and made all the more so
by the hint of controversy in the other disciplines just as we have in
our own psychoanalytic one. This is evident in the academic anatomical world (Chapter Two) and complicates the search for any definite
conclusions. I hope that the ways in which I have made use of their
findings offers creative sense.

There are various other reasons I can think of that brought things
together at this time, but I will just choose one here which is relevant to
my themes. Certain events in life can lead to a creative surge. In March,
I was invited on a trip to Sicily, where I had always wanted to go. I knew
very little about it, only a pull to explore more of Italy and maybe living
on an island makes for an interest in other islands. Perhaps the current
troubles of the mass migration that have been centred there contributed
to a wish to understand more about the history and the many consecu-
tive invasions of Greeks, Romans, Arabs, and others, up to the present
day. Meanwhile, the delights of Sicily were unbounded. The beauty, the
culture, the warmth, all served to provide pleasure and fulfilment. Why
do I include it here? Because of a dream I had later, in the week before
going to see the Sicily exhibition at the British Museum in June. It was
a very vivid dream about

> the Triskelion, from the Greek meaning "three-legged", the
> triangular-shaped motif or image that is seen all over Sicily, resem-
> bling the shape of the island itself and standing for Eternity. There
> is the face of a woman at the centre and a foot on each corner, giv-
> ing the impression that it bowls along. In the dream there was an
> expectation that I had to put this in my book.

On waking, though the sense of conviction remained, I could not think
why or how this should be so; it seemed like nonsense. But giving it
some thought, I decided that the connection was to the shape of the
mother's body, but that it would still not really fit into the book. Looking
at the Triskelion at the exhibition, my friend thought it was a Christian

image of the Trinity: Father, Son, and the Holy Ghost. Maybe, but I thought of the Oedipus complex: father, mother, and baby. I realised that it belonged in the book, here in my Afterthoughts, as an image of creativity.

Another meaning that might be attributed to the Triskelion is of ego, superego, and id. An important task for the analyst can be thought of as always aiming to sit at the central point of the three parts of the mind, ego, superego, and id, when listening and responding to patients (an idea attributed to David Tuckett, personal communication Sara Flanders). Perhaps women, in view of the hidden-ness of their sexual make-up, the Triskelion being seen as the mother's body, are at an advantage with the integration required (Brierley's original idea, Chapter Three). Men call upon their feminine side psychically.

I always wished my parents had named me Anna, not Anne. It would have been more interesting, less vague. To return to Sicily, I remember seeing, right in the centre of the island, high on a hilltop, the ancient city of Enna. Would that have been an alternative? But they did add Rosemary, like my mother, and though as a child I hated it, later I came to value it. At the British Museum exhibition, after the dream, I thought of my beginning, right in the middle of her body, the Triskelion. I think of the Triskelion as the mother's body and that it does belong in this book. I am thankful for my dream.

Legend has it that the abduction of Persephone by Hades, the god of the Underworld, took place near Enna in central Sicily. Sanctuaries were built all over Sicily in honour of Persephone and her mother Demeter, for people to give offerings back to the earth. Therefore, I see my book as an offering back to the earth.

NOTES

Preface

1. Zachary, A. (1986). A new look at the vulnerability of puerperal mothers. *Psychoanalytic Psychotherapy, 1*: 71–89.
2. Zachary, A. (2002). The menopause: dignity and development at the end of the reproductive cycle. *Psychoanalytic Psychotherapy, 16*: 20–36.
3. Zachary, A. (2000). Uneasy triangles: a brief overview of the history of homosexuality. *British Journal of Psychotherapy, 17*: 489–492.
4. Gillespie, W. H. (1969). Concepts of vaginal orgasm. *International Journal of Psycho-Analysis, 50*: 495–497.
5. O'Connell, H., et al. (1998). Anatomical relationship between clitoris and urethra. *Journal of Urology, 159*: 1892–1897.
6. Tyson, P. (2003). Some psychoanalytic perspectives on women. *International Journal of Psycho-Analysis, 51*(4): 1119–1126.
7. "Homologue" meaning an organ that has the same relation, proportion, relative position, or that corresponds to the other organ.
8. Van Turnhout, A., et al. (1995). The female corpus spongiosum re-visited. *Acta Obstetricia et Gynecologica Scandinavica, 74*: 767–771.

Chapter Two

1. "Homologue" meaning an organ that has the same relation, proportion, relative position, or that corresponds to the other organ.
2. There is a rather lurid schematic diagram of the clitoris in three dimensions from O'Connell's website. This offers less, in my view, than the shadowy representation of the "hidden-ness" of Figure 2.
3. "Perivaginal" means surrounding the vagina.
4. What is very disappointing, but yet in line with the theme running through this book, is that the work of Masters and Johnson has now been removed from the open shelves of two London libraries I have frequented. In one, they are in storage; the other, I fear, has disposed of them—the excuse, lack of space.
5. According to Appignanesi and Forrester, Princess Marie Bonaparte herself had a series of operations to move her clitoris nearer to her vagina. This is of historical importance, perhaps just the forerunner to the "routine hysterectomy" of today in terms of incredulity. Despite this rather concrete endeavour, paradoxically, it was she who was at the same time largely responsible for the promotion and acceptance of psychoanalysis throughout France.

Chapter Three

1. This list leaves out Lacan (1972), whom I have added to my grid. Passing reference is made to Lacan in other sections of the book.
2. I discovered recently when reading *The Female Body* (2013, edited by Moeslein-Teising & Thomson Salo) that there was a poster at the Chicago International Conference in 2009 by Dr A. Bilger on which he recognised that "These psychoanalytical discoveries and wisdom were, however, periodically ignored or forgotten". His poster was visual, with drawings of the ancient Venus of Ulm (the cover picture of *The Female Body*), a forerunner to my putting into words how the history mirrors the anatomy.

Chapter Four

1. This patient was treated as part of the Anna Freud Centre Young Adults' Research Project (1992–1998).

2. Janine Chasseguet-Smirgel, (1964) *Recherches psychoanalytiques nouvelles sur la sexualite feminine,* and *Female sexuality.*
3. Freud approached femininity in terms of the body and penis envy, whilst Jones focused on the feminine need for the love of the object.
4. This material is presented here with the permission of the patient but also with her help since she has drawn the illustrations of the dolls.

Chapter Five

1. Ironically, more recently oestrogen has been also considered carcinogenic for some people, depending on gene profile, and it is given generally more cautiously. Hormone replacement therapy (HRT) is now limited to five years in case it could cause cancer.
2. This organisation has since divided into the British Psychoanalytic Association (BPA) affiliated to the International Psychoanalytic Association (IPA) and its psychotherapy section amalgamated with other organisations into the British Psychotherapy Foundation (BPF).
3. In this new age of LGBT politics, many organisations are having to spend money on removing gender-specific labelling, and toilets have become unisex.
4. Mr P was my designated research patient in the long-running "violence workshop" at the Portman Clinic which examined the differences between self-preservative (ruthless) violence and sado-masochistic violence.

Chapter Six

1. Zachary, A. (1986). A new look at the vulnerability of puerperal mothers. *Psychoanalytic Psychotherapy, 1*: 71–89; and in *The Family as Inpatient.* London: Free Association Books.

Chapter Seven

1. I read Monique Cournut-Janin, then Raphael-Leff, and then Alizade. In doing so, I discovered that they had all three worked together for a time on COWAP (Committee on Women and Psychoanalysis) before the sad death of Alizade.

2. The chronology here seems disrupted, this work appearing now and not in Chapter Nine, "Recent developments". But Cournut-Janin was writing originally in French in 1996.
3. And even in the *British Medical Journal* (23 July 2016) in a surgical article on pelvic organ prolapse (M. Barber).

Chapter Eight

1. This example is taken from some time ago, before the clinic acquired its current larger and excellent child psychotherapy team.
2. This material is presented here with the permission of the patient but also with her help since she has drawn the illustrations of the dolls.
3. My thanks to Marie Saba for introducing me to this new work.

Chapter Nine

1. In retrospect this book is not finished. It warrants a chapter on "Eating disorders," maybe in a second edition.

REFERENCES

Aaronovitch D. (1997). Unwanted orgasms. *The Independent* 23/12/97.

Abraham, K. (1920). The female castration complex. In: *Selected Papers on Psychoanalysis*. London: Hogarth Press.

Abram, J. (2007). *The Language of Winnicott: A Dictionary of Winnicott's Use of Words*. London: Karnac.

Alizade, A. M. (1999). *Feminine Sensuality*. London: Karnac.

Alizade, A. M. (2003). *Studies on Femininity*. London: Karnac.

Alizade, A. M. (2006). *Motherhood in the Twenty-First Century*. London: Karnac.

Andahazi, F. (1996). *The Anatomist*. London: Doubleday.

Anderson, R. (Ed.) (1992). *Clinical Lectures on Klein and Bion*. London: Routledge, The New Library of Psychoanalysis.

Angier, N. (1999). *Woman*. London: Virago.

Appignanesi, L., & Forrester, J. (1992). *Freud's Women*. London: Weidenfeld & Nicolson.

Arden, M. (1987). A concept of femininity: Sylvia Payne's 1935 paper reassessed. *International Review of Psycho-Analysis, 14*: 237–244.

Atlas, G. (2016). *The Enigma of Desire*. London: Routledge.

Babuscio, J. (1978). The cinema of camp. *Gay Sunshine*, Summer: 18–21.

Balsam, R. (1996). The pregnant mother and the body image of the daughter. *Journal of the American Psychoanalytical Association, 44* (Suppl): 401–427.

Balsam, R. (2003). The vanished pregnant body. *Journal of the American Psychoanalytical Association, 51/4*: 1153–1179.

Balsam, R. (2012). *Women's Bodies in Psychoanalysis*. New York: Routledge.

Barber, M. (2016). Pelvic organ prolapse. *British Medical Journal*, 23 July: 159–162.

Bemesderfer, S. (1996). A revised psychoanalytic view of the menopause. *Journal of the American Psychoanalytic Association, 44* (Suppl): 351–369.

Birksted-Breen, D. (1989). Working with an anorexic patient. *International Journal of Psycho-Analysis, 70*: 29–40.

Birksted-Breen, D. (1993). *The Gender Conundrum*. London: Routledge.

Birksted-Breen, D. (1996). Phallus, penis, and mental space. *International Journal of Psycho-Analysis, 77*: 649–657.

Birksted-Breen, D., Flanders, S., & Gibault, A. (Eds.) (2010). *Reading French Psychoanalysis*. London: Routledge, The New Library of Psychoanalysis.

Blau, A. (1943). A philological note on a defect in sex organ nomenclature. *Psychoanalytic Quarterly, 12*: 481–485.

Bollas, C. (2011). *The Christopher Bollas Reader*. London: Routledge.

Brash, J. C. (Ed.) (1953). *Cunningham's Textbook of Anatomy*. London: Oxford University Press, 1981.

Brierley, M. (1932). Some problems of integration in women. *International Journal of Psycho-Analysis, 13*: 433–448.

Budd, S., & Rusbridger, R. (Eds.) (2005). *Introducing Psychoanalysis*. London: Routledge.

Burton, A. (1996). The meaning of perineal activity in women: an inner sphinx. *Journal of the American Psychoanalytic Association, 44* (Suppl): 241–259.

Chasseguet-Smirgel, J. (1964). *Recherches psychoanalytiques nouvelles sur la sexualite feminine*. Paris: Editions Payot. [Published in English as *Female Sexuality*. London: Virago, 1981.]

Chodorow, N. (1992). Heterosexuality as a compromise formation: reflections on the psychoanalytic theory of sexual development. *Psychoanalysis and Contemporary Thought, 15*: 267–304.

Chodorow, N. (2003). "Too late": ambivalence about motherhood. *Journal of the American Psychoanalytical Association, 51(4)*: 1181–1198.

Christopher, E. (1996). A century of sex: developments in analytic thinking as attitudes in society change. Monograph No. 8, British Association of Psychotherapists.

Cournut-Janin, M. (1998). The feminine and femininity. In: D. Birksted-Breen, S. Flanders, & A. Gibault (Eds.), *Reading French Psychoanalysis*. London: Routledge, The New Library of Psychoanalysis, 2010.

Cournut-Janin, M. (2003). Aux origines femininities de la sexualite [On the female origins of sexuality] by Jacques Andre. Paris: Presses Univ. France, 1995. *International Journal of Psycho-Analysis, 84*: 1639–1642.

Crowley Jack, D. (1999). *Behind the Mask: Destruction and Creativity in Women's Aggression.* Cambridge, MA: Harvard University Press.

Deutsch, H. (1945). *The Psychology of Women.* New York: Grune & Stratton.

Dorsey, D. (1996). Castration anxiety or genital anxiety? *Journal of the American Psychoanalytic Association, 44* (Suppl.): 283–302.

Ebenstein, J. (2016). *The Anatomical Venus.* London: Thames & Hudson.

Elise, D. (1997). Primary femininity, bisexuality and the female ego ideal: a re-examination of female developmental theory. *Psychoanalytic Quarterly, 66*: 489–517.

Freud, S. (1905d). *Three Essays on the Theory of Sexuality, S. E., 7*: 125–248.

Freud, S. (1910c). *Leonardo da Vinci and a Memory of his Childhood, S. E., 11*: 59–138.

Freud, S. (1920g). *Beyond the Pleasure Principle, S. E., 18*: 7–64.

Freud, S. (1923b). *The Ego and the Id, S. E., 19*: 3–63.

Freud, S. (1925j). Some psychical consequences of the anatomical distinction between the sexes. *S. E., 19*: 243–260.

Freud, S. (1926e). *The Question of Lay Analysis, S. E., 20*: 183–250.

Freud, S. (1931b). Female sexuality, *S. E., 21*: 221–246.

Freud, S. (1933a). *New Introductory Lectures on Psycho-Analysis*: Femininity, *S. E., 22*: 112–135.

Gibeault, A. (1988). On the feminine and the masculine: afterthoughts on Jacqueline Cosnier's book *Destins de la femininite.* In: D. Birksted-Breen (Ed.), *The Gender Conundrum.* London: Routledge, 1993.

Gillepsie, W. (1956). The general theory of sexual perversion. *International Journal of Psycho-Analysis, 37*: 396–403.

Gillespie, W. (1969). Concepts of vaginal orgasm. *International Journal of Psycho-Analysis, 50*: 495–497. [Reprinted in D. Birksted-Breen (Ed.), *The Gender Conundrum.* London: Routledge, 1993.]

Gillespie, W. (1975). Woman and her discontents. In: *The British School of Psychoanalysis: The Independent Tradition.* London: Free Association Books, 1986.

Gilmore, K. (1998). Cloacal anxiety in female development. *Journal of the American Psychoanalytic Association, 46*: 443–470.

Glasser, M. (1979). Some aspects of the role of aggression in perversions. In: I. Rosen (Ed.), *Sexual Deviation.* Oxford: Oxford University Press.

Greenacre, P. (1964). A study on the nature of inspiration. 1: Some special considerations regarding the phallic phase. *Journal of the American Psychoanalytic Association, 12*: 6–31.

Grunberger, B. (1964). Outline for a study of narcissism in female sexuality. In: J. Chasseguet-Smirgel (Ed.), *Female Sexuality.* London: Virago, 1981.

Holtzman, D., & Kulish, N. (2003). Feminisation of the female Oedipus complex. *Journal of the American Psychoanalytical Association, 51(4)*: 1127–1151.

116   REFERENCES

Horney, K. (1924). On the genesis of the castration complex in women. *International Journal of Psycho-Analysis, 5*: 50–65.

Jones, E. (1927). The early development of female sexuality. *International Journal of Psycho-Analysis, 8*: 459–472.

Jones, E. (1933). Early female sexuality. *International Journal of Psycho-Analysis, 16*: 263–273.

Klein, M. (1928). Early stages of the Oedipus complex. *International Journal of Psycho-Analysis, 9*: 167–180.

Klein, M. (1975). *Envy and Gratitude, and Other Works 1946–1963.* London: The Hogarth Press and the Institute of Psychoanalysis.

Kohon, G. (2000). *No Lost Certainties To Be Recovered.* London: Karnac.

Kohon, G. (2016). *Reflections on the Aesthetic Experience.* London: Routledge.

Kramer Richards, A. (2003). A fresh look at perversion. *Journal of the American Psychoanalytical Association, 51*(4): 1119–1218.

Kulish, N. (1991). The mental representation of the clitoris. *Psychoanalytic Inquiry, 11*: 511–536.

Kulish, N. (2000). Primary femininity: clinical advances and theoretical ambiguities. *Journal of the American Psychoanalytic Association, 48*: 1355–1379.

Lacan, J. (1972–1973). God and the jouissance of the woman: a love letter. Seminar XX, Encore. [Translated in *Feminine Sexuality.*]

Lerner, H. (1976). Parental mislabelling of female genitals as a determinant of penis envy and learning inhibitions in women. *Journal of the American Psychoanalytic Association, 24* (Suppl.): 269–283.

Luckhurst, P. (2016). Reclaiming the biscuit. *Evening Standard.* London, 30 September.

Maier, T. (2009). *Masters of Sex.* London: Basic Books.

Masters, W., & Johnston, V. (1966). *Human Sexual Response.* New York: Little, Brown & Co.

McDougall, J. (1972). Primal scene and sexual perversion. *International Journal of Psycho-Analysis, 53*: 371.

Melnick, B. (1997). Metaphor and the theory of libidinal development. *International Journal of Psycho-Analysis, 78*: 997–1016.

Mitchell, J. (1974). *Psychoanalysis and Feminism.* London: Allen Lane.

Mitchell, J., & Rose, J. (1982). *Feminine Sexuality: Introductions I & II.* London: Macmillan Press.

Montgrain, N. (1983). On the vicissitudes of female sexuality: the difficult path from "anatomical destiny" to psychic representation. *International Journal of Psycho-Analysis, 64*: 169–186.

Montrelay, M. (1970). *Recherches sur la femininite.* Critique translated in P. Adams, & E. Cowie, (Eds.), *The Woman in Question M/F.* Boston: MIT Press, 1990. [Reprinted as Inquiry into femininity. Translated in D. Birksted-Breen (Ed.), *The Gender Conundrum.* London: Routledge, 1993.]

Motz, A. (2001). *The Psychology of Female Violence: Crimes against the Body*. London: Brunner.

O'Connell, H., et al. (1998). Anatomical relationship between clitoris and urethra. *Journal of Urology, 159*: 1892–1897.

O'Connell, H., et al. (2005a). Clitoral anatomy in nulliparous, healthy, premenopausal volunteers using unenhanced magnetic resonance imaging. *Journal of Urology, 173*: 2060–2063.

O'Connell, H., et al. (2005b). Anatomy of the clitoris. *Journal of Urology, 174*: 1189–1195.

O'Connell, H., et al. (2008). The anatomy of the distal vagina: towards unity. *Journal of Sexual Medicine, 5*: 1883–1891.

O'Connor, S. (2014). Learning from women with psychoses. *Psychoanalytic Psychotherapy, 28*(2): 159–175.

O'Dent, M. (2004). Return of the French revolutionary. *Guardian 2*: Health, 9 March, p. 14.

Olds, S. (2016). *Odes*. New York: Alfred. A. Knopf.

Parsons, M. (2000a). *The Dove that Returns, the Dove that Vanishes*. London: Routledge, The New Library of Psychoanalysis.

Parsons, M. (2000b). Sexuality and perversion a hundred years on: discovering what Freud discovered. *International Journal of Psychoanalysis, 81*: 37–51.

Payne, S. (1935). A concept of femininity. *British Journal of Medical Psychology, 15*: 18–33.

Perelberg, R. (2015). *Murdered Father, Dead Father*. London: Routledge, The New Library of Psychoanalysis.

Pines, D. (1993). *A Woman's Unconscious Use of Her Body*. London: Virago Press.

Raphael-Leff, J. (1993). *Pregnancy: The Inside Story*. London: The Sheldon Press. [Reprinted London: Karnac, 2003.]

Raphael-Leff, J. (2000). *Spilt Milk: Perinatal Loss and Breakdown*. London: Karnac.

Raphael-Leff, J., & Perelberg, R. (2008). *Female Experience*. London: The Anna Freud Centre, Routledge.

Reading P. J. & Will R. G. (1997). Unwanted orgasms. *The Lancet* 13/12/97.

Rees, M., O'Connell, H., et al. (2000). The suspensory ligaments of the clitoris: connective tissue supports of the erectile tissues of the female urogenital region. *Clinical Anatomy, 13*: 397–403.

Rosenbaum, R. (1995). *The Independent*. London, 27 January.

Sachs, H. (1923). "Zur Genese der Perversionen" *Int. Zeitschr. f. Psychoanal, 9*: 172.

Schuker, E., & Levinson, N. (1991). *Female Psychology: An Annotated Bibliography*. Penryn: The Atlantic Press.

Segal, H. (1957). Notes on symbol formation. In: *The Work of Hanna Segal*. New York: Jason Aronson, 1981.

Sherfey, M. J. (1966). The evolution and nature of female sexuality in relation to psychoanalytic theory. *Journal of the American Psychoanalytical Association, 14*: 28–128.

Sontag, S. (1964). Notes on "Camp". *Partisan Review, 30*: 515–530.

Spillius, E., et al. (2011). *A New Dictionary of Kleinian Thought*. London: Routledge.

Stoller, R. (1968). The sense of femaleness. *Psychoanalytic Quarterly, 37*: 42–55.

Symington, N. (2002). *A Pattern of Madness*. London: Karnac.

Thomson Salo, F., & Moeslein-Teising, I. (Eds.) (2003). *The Female Body*. London: Karnac.

Toesca, A., et al. (1996). Immunohistochemical study of the corpus cavernosa of the human clitoris. *Journal of Anatomy, 188*: 513–520.

Tyson, P. (2003). Some psychoanalytic perspectives on women. *International Journal of Psycho-Analysis, 51*(4): 1119–1126.

Van Turnhout, A., et al. (1995). The female corpus spongiosum re-visited. *Acta Obstetricia et Gynecologica Scandinavica, 74*: 767–771.

Waddell, M. (2002). *Inside Lives: Psychoanalysis and the Growth of the Personality*. London: Tavistock Series, Karnac. [First edition, London: Duckworth, 1998.]

Welldon, E. (1988). *Mother, Madonna, Whore: The Idealisation and Denigration of Motherhood*. London: Free Association Books.

Wilson, E. (1998). *Consilience: The Unity of Knowledge*. London: Little, Brown, & Co.

Winnicott, D. W. (1971). *Playing and Reality*. London: Penguin Books.

Young-Bruehl, E. (Ed.) (1990). *Freud on Women: A Reader*. London: Hogarth Press.

Zachary, A. (1986). A new look at the vulnerability of puerperal mothers. *Psychoanalytic Psychotherapy, 1*: 71–89.

Zachary, A. (1996). Bisexuality: a universal phenomenon. In: *A Century of Sex: Developments in Analytic Thinking as Attitudes in Society Change*. Monograph No. 8. British Association of Psychotherapists.

Zachary, A. (2000). Uneasy triangles: a brief overview of the history of homosexuality. *British Journal of Psychotherapy, 17*: 489–492.

Zachary, A. (2002). The menopause: dignity and development at the end of the reproductive cycle. *Psychoanalytic Psychotherapy, 16*: 20–36.

Zemon, N., & Arfarge, A. (1995). *A History of Women: Renaissance and Enlightenment Paradoxes*. Cambridge, MA: Harvard University Press.

INDEX

Aaronovitch, D., xxiv
Abject, xxiv, 40, 72
Abraham, K., xxv
Abram, J., 74
adreno-genital insensitivity syndrome
    (AIS), 54–56
aggression in boys, 88
AIS. *See* adreno-genital insensitivity
    syndrome
Alizade, A. M., 83, 84, 101, 111
Anatomical Venus, The, 8–9
anatomical wax model, 9–10
Anatomist, The, 5
Andahazi, F., 5–6
androgen insufficiency syndrome
    (AIS), xxvii, 4
Angier, N., xxiv, 11, 54, 87, 96
    development of gender
        difference, 54
    mosaic imagination, 56
    testicular feminization, 54–55
Anziou, D., 83
Appignanesi, L., 110

Arden, M., 32, 34
Atlas, G., 49, 51, 92, 104

Babuscio, J., 67
Balsam, R., xxviii, 40, 102
BAP. *See* British Association of
    Psychotherapists
Barber, M., 112
Bemesderfer, S., 33
Benedek, xxv, 3
"benign" aggression, 87
Birksted-Breen, D., 13, 17, 25, 34, 40,
    41, 46, 58, 104
    duality in Freud's theory of
        sexuality, 46
    out-of-focusness, 59, 61
    penis-as-link, 49, 50
bisexuality, xxvii, 53
    AIS, 54–56
    case histories, 62–69
    concept of "camp", 64
    development of gender difference, 54
    gender, 58

119

O'Connell, H., xxiii, 5, 14, 16, 17,
        35, 109
    research, 19
O'Connor, S., xxviii, 88
Odent, M., 93
Odent's theory. *See* theories of natural
        birth
Oedipus complex, 60
Olds, S., 83, 103
"ordinary" aggression, 87
orgasm
    female, 19
    male and female psyche at, 34

Parker, 34, 35
Parsons, M., xxiii, 13, 41, 82
    description of Freud's conception
        of Oedipus complex, 34
Payne, S., 32, 34
penis-as-link, 49, 50
penis/vagina imbalance, 31
Perelberg, R., xxiv, 20, 40, 57, 72, 81,
        82, 88, 101
perivaginal, 110
    spongioform tissue, 18
phallus, 49
Pines, D., 31
Pontalis, 58
primary femininity, 32–33
primary repression of vagina, 82–83
psychic bisexuality, 53 *see also*:
        bisexuality
psychoanalysis, xxix
    theory of female sexuality, xxv
psychoanalytic literatures on female
        sexuality, 26–30
psychoanalytic theories, xxxi
psychoanalytic theory of female
        sexuality, 25
    early classical work, 31
    faulty concept of female sexuality,
        31
    feminine genital anxiety, 34
    femininity as "integration", 32
    frames of reference used in, 33
    "Freud–Jones" debate, 31

integrative aspect of feminine
        thinking, 34
male and female psyche at orgasm,
        34
modern theories, 31–32
Parson's description of Freud's
        conception of Oedipus
        complex, 34
primary femininity, 32–33
shown as grid, 26–30
structures linked with clitoris, 35
psychoanalytic theory of female
        sexuality, 3

Raphael-Leff, J., 56, 57, 80, 111
Reading French Psychoanalysis, 79
Rees, M., 16
Riviere, J., 80
Rose, J., xxv
Rosenbaum, R., 60
routine hysterectomy, 110
Rusbridger, R., 25

Sachs, H., xxx, 60
Salo, 101
sanctioned voyeurism, 8
Schuker, E., xxv, 25
Schulman, 17
sex, 71
Sheldon posture-photo phenomenon,
        60
Sheldon, W. H., 60
Shengold, 88
Sherfey, M. J., 19, 20
Sontag, S., 64, 67
spasms, 34
spinning, 34
Stoller, R., 32
Susini, Clemente, 9
Symington, N., 33

testicular feminization. *See* adreno-
        genital insensitivity
        syndrome
theories of natural birth, 93
theory of female sexuality, xxv